A
SUPERLATIVE
PALETTE
CONTEMPORARY BLACK WOMEN ARTISTS

A
SUPERLATIVE
PALETTE
CONTEMPORARY
BLACK WOMEN
ARTISTS

CURATED BY
DEXTER WIMBERLY

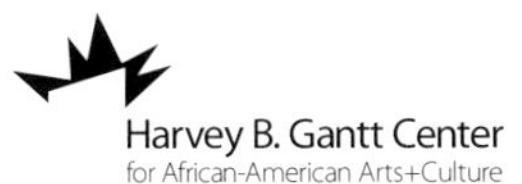

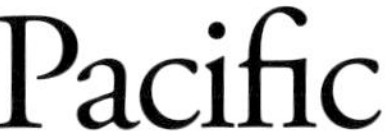

With *A Superlative Palette: Contemporary Black Women Artists*, the Harvey B. Gantt Center has assembled the work of twelve internationally renowned makers who are among the most powerful in the art world today. In the realm of contemporary art, the contributions of Black women artists have been transformative, enriching the cultural landscape and challenging traditional narratives.

The collages, paintings, and sculpture included in this exhibition encompass a broad range of themes and styles. The works are not only stunning but also foreground representation as these artists advocate for social justice, equality, and empowerment.

Historically, Black women creatives have faced marginalization and underrepresentation. Despite obstacles, these talented women have pushed past boundaries, demanding their rightful place in the canon.

A number of the works included in *A Superlative Palette* are portraits of women in repose, at leisure. The subject's gaze is often direct and unflinching – emblematic, I believe, of the self-assurance that these twelve artists possess.

The most prominent work, *Clarivel Face Forward Gazing* (2024), was created for this exhibition by multidisciplinary artist Mickalene Thomas and is on view to the public for the first time. Thomas is known for her elaborate portraits of Black women. At eight by twelve feet and bedazzled, the mixed media work commands attention, drawing the viewer in to appreciate the intricate detail.

Deborah Roberts' near life-sized collages of children moving through the world in innocence are presented alongside the frenetic energy of Nina Chanel Abney's *Always Ready, Always There* (2018).

Requiem for my Navigator (2021), painter Calida Rawles' ethereal portrait of a man's face submerged in water, can evoke either terror or peace. This is the beauty of this collection of works. The stories we walk away with, after viewing the exhibition, are dependent upon the stories and experiences we bring.

We are thankful to the curator, Dexter Wimberly. The confluence of his unique insight, expertise, and passion fashioned this thought-provoking palette of works.

I am also grateful to the Gantt Center Board of Directors, staff, and volunteers, whose commitment to excellence ensures the long-term success of our institution.

Lastly, we are indebted to the artists, the brilliant visionaries whose work inspires us.

— Bonita Buford, *President & CEO*
Harvey B. Gantt Center for African-American Arts + Culture

A SUPERLATIVE PALETTE: CONTEMPORARY BLACK WOMEN ARTISTS

Dexter Wimberly

A Superlative Palette brings together the work of twelve generation-defining, contemporary Black women artists from around the world. In the realm of contemporary art, the contributions of Black women artists have been transformative, challenging traditional narratives and enriching the cultural landscape. Their powerful and thought-provoking work has not only redefined artistic expression but also played a significant role in advocating for social justice, equality, and empowerment. Black women artists have historically faced marginalization and underrepresentation within the art world. Despite these obstacles, they have persevered and crafted an artistry that encompasses a diverse range of themes, mediums, and styles.

Artists in the exhibition include Nina Chanel Abney, ruby onyinyechi amanze, Lauren Halsey, Rachel Jones, Toyin Ojih Odutola, Jennifer Packer, Calida Rawles, Deborah Roberts, Tschabalala Self, Amy Sherald, Mickalene Thomas, and Lynette Yiadom-Boakye.

Combining representation and abstraction, Nina Chanel Abney's paintings capture the frenetic pace of contemporary culture. Broaching subjects as diverse as race, celebrity culture, religion, politics, sex, and art history, her works eschew linear storytelling in lieu of disjointed narratives. ruby onyinyechi amanze composes drawings that defy the two-dimensional bounds of paper. Her objects float across the pages, untethered from indicators of gravity, space, or time. All the forms are free from the restrictions of land, all sense of directionality is lost, and they are light and unbounded.

Artist Lauren Halsey is rethinking the possibilities for art, architecture, and community engagement. Halsey's work maintains a sense of civic urgency and free-flowing imagination, reflecting the lives of the people and places around her and addressing the crucial issues confronting people of color, queer populations, and the working class. In her paintings, Rachel Jones grapples with the challenges of finding visual means to convey abstract, existential concepts. The figures in her work are notably abstracted, and Jones uses bold color, competing forms, and an interplay of textures to communicate her ideas to viewers, who bring their own experiences and cultural backgrounds to the interpretation of her works.

Interested in the topography of skin, Toyin Ojih Odutola has a distinctive style of mark-making using only basic drawing materials, such as ballpoint pens, pencils, pastels, and charcoal. This signature technique involves building up layers on the page, through blending and shading with the highest level of detail, creating compositions that reinvent and reinterpret the traditions of portraiture. Jennifer Packer's paintings are rendered in loose line and brushstroke using a limited color palette, often to the extent that her subject merges with or retreats into the background. Suggesting an emotional and psychological depth, her work is enigmatic, avoiding a straightforward reading.

The paintings of Calida Rawles merge hyper-realism with poetic abstraction. Situating her subjects in dynamic spaces, her recent work employs water as a vital, organic, multifaceted material and historically charged space. Deborah Roberts focuses her gaze on Black children—historically, and still today, among the most vulnerable members of our population—investigating how societal pressures, projected images of beauty or masculinity, and the violence of American racism condition their experiences growing up in this country as well as how others perceive them.

The formal and conceptual aspects of Tschabalala Self's work seek to expand her critical inquiry into selfhood and human flourishing. The figures in her work take up space on large pieces of paper or colorful canvases and seem to be caught in private, joyous moments: dancing with a lover, reclining on a bed, greeting a friend. Subverting the genre of portraiture and challenging accepted notions of American identity, Amy Sherald attempts to restore a broader, fuller picture of humanity. Sherald's work thus foregrounds the idea that Black life and identity are not solely tethered to grappling publicly with social issues and that resistance lies equally in a full interior life and an expansive vision of selfhood in the world.

Mickalene Thomas introduces complex notions of femininity and challenges common definitions of beauty and aesthetic representation. Her work stems from her long study of art history and classical genres of portraiture and landscape. Lynette Yiadom-Boakye creates fictional figures that are untethered from a specific time or place and are born from various untraceable subjects: people, objects, thoughts, photographs, or images she has drawn, observed, or recalled. This lack of fixed narrative reference leaves her work open to the projected imagination of the viewer.

A SHARED SENSIBILITY OF THE BLACK FEMININE
Kalia Brooks, PhD

A Superlative Palette, curated by Dexter Wimberly, gives the viewer an opportunity to learn anew about the vast contributions Black women artists from the African diaspora have made to the visual canon of contemporary art. This thoughtful selection of work that includes painting, collage, drawing, mixed media, and sculpture epitomizes the contributions of these artists in representing the dynamics of Black life within the broader context of visual culture. Each of the artists expresses in their work the importance of implementing a radical approach to imaging the complexity and depth of the Black subject and Black subjectivity in art and culture at large. Moreover, each artist's distinct articulation imbues the artwork with transformative character and abstract dimension for other imaginaries to emerge. The stories that resonate through these compositions signify the texture of the communities they depict. Whether the focus be on objects, artifacts, people, landscapes, protests, folklore, or enviroments, these artists are concerned with the forms, figures, and events that elucidate the qualities of the contemporary Black experience.

Mickalene Thomas, Deborah Roberts, and Tschabalala Self show the viewer how the image of the Black female body can intervene in the complexity of the gaze. Their work implores the viewer to look. The gaze is serene, reflexive, and critical as it confronts, side-eyes, and questions the audience. Their subjects claim the right of representation as they assert their self-assuredness, beauty, and pleasure. When images of Black women become the subject, as in the work of Toyin Ojih Odutola and Lynette Yiadom-Boakye, they signify opportunity, uplift, protection, and self-governance. In this way, the individual is a surrogate for the collective – activating a shared sensibility of the Black feminine. The Black female body becomes the figure through which the value of the human condition is emphasized. These stunning depictions reveal history, personal memory, biography, and art-historical references in service of the re-creation and construction of the self. These artists realign our attention to the power of Black figuration. Amy Sherald's portrait, for example, heralds the whimsical banality of the subject. She imbues the figure with a softness symbolized by his gentle grasp of a rabbit, which is a visual metaphor for the artist's careful protection of the delicacy and proliferation of Black life.

While the Black figure remains powerful as a subversive trope, other artists have developed a set of aesthetic principles to absent the body. Rachel Jones' and Jennifer Packer's use of abstract form and its interrelated components highlights the relationship of the body within a system – the ways the system constricts the body and the ways the body can manipulate, transform, and create tension within a system. In doing so, Jones and Packer help viewers understand how exchange, materials, and process become a currency by which new associations of subjective experience are formed. This kind of artwork is engaged with issues relating to belonging, dislocation, and nodes of connectivity. It calls attention to the layering of social and cultural information that prescribes the body with codes of signification. This work, therefore, becomes a mode by which to express the combination of biological and cultural factors that shape human experience and ultimately call upon the visual sense of the body to relate to and move through time and space. Central to this kind of art making is an exploration of other forms of beauty and alternative modes of representation. Rather than perceiving the form of the body, these images encourage viewers to think beyond the limits of the biological self into realms that translate the concept of Blackness into the metaphysical terms of frequency, energy, and vibration.

The space in between figuration and abstraction is a powerful zone in which to explore the migratory experience of the African diaspora. Rather than depicting the actual passage of migration, ruby onyinyechi amanze and Calida Rawles show the viewer segments of the body in motion. Their work expounds upon the discourse of migration by generating a visual language that represents the millions of individuals and families who have preserved tradition, created new culture, and maintained dignity in the face of profound dislocation. Their distinct perspectives underscore the sensations of identifying the self and community in the context of social and cultural transit.

The artists in this exhibition are challenging the brute force that popular culture and visual history have on the bodies and minds of Black people. By reclaiming power over the images that seep into the consciousness of Black people through the built environment and in popular media, as seen in the work of Lauren Halsey and Nina Chanel Abney, these artists encourage the viewer to think critically about the inheritance of Black representation and the infinitude of Black futures. The personal spaces they access, which are typically veiled from public view, become a critical site of engagement for ideas related to beauty, self-fashioning, public expectation, and personal subversion within the larger context of the history of visual representation.

Wimberly's keen eye for and cultivated knowledge of the artists included in the exhibition are an exercise in curatorial storytelling through art that conveys a sense of comfort between him and his subject matter. The artistic endeavor is as much personal as it is political, and it is political on the most personal level. The artists and curator take a big idea, like that of *visibility*, and seek out the places where most people would not look to reveal that the politics of visibility are at work every day in our mundane actions. These artists lean into the agency that is inherent in how we choose to appear in the world. Through art, the viewer learns there is not a singular vision of the Black subject. These women are at the forefront of reconsidering the perceptible embodiments of race, gender, nationality, and a number of other social identity positions. They prompt the viewer to think not only about the history of representation but also about the present ways art functions to reform previously limited scopes of perceptibility and the implications that these expanded definitions have on future generations of Black folks.

PLATES

NINA CHANEL ABNEY

Combining representation and abstraction, Nina Chanel Abney's paintings capture the frenetic pace of contemporary culture. Broaching subjects as diverse as race, celebrity culture, religion, politics, sex, and art history, her works eschew linear storytelling in lieu of disjointed narratives. The effect is information overload, balanced with a kind of spontaneous order, where time and space are compressed and identity is interchangeable. Through a bracing use of color and unapologetic scale, Abney's canvases propose a new type of history painting, one grounded in the barrage of everyday events and funneled through the velocity of the internet. Her distinctively bold style harnesses the flux and simultaneity that has come to define life in the twenty-first century.

Abney (b. Harvey, IL; lives and works in New York, NY) had her first solo museum exhibition, *Nina Chanel Abney: Royal Flush*, in 2017 at the Nasher Museum of Art, Durham, NC. It traveled to the Chicago Cultural Center and then to Los Angeles, where it was jointly presented by the Institute of Contemporary Art (ICA) and the California African American Museum. The final venue for the exhibition was the Neuberger Museum of Art, Purchase College, State University of New York. The exhibition is accompanied by a comprehensive, fully illustrated, hardcover catalogue with critical essays by the exhibition curator, Marshall Price, as well as Jamillah James, curator at the ICA, Los Angeles; Natalie Y. Moore, a South Side bureau reporter for Chicago Public Media, WBEZ; and Richard J. Powell, professor of Art and Art History at Duke University, Durham, NC. Her work is included in collections around the world, including the Brooklyn Museum, the Rubell Family Collection, the Bronx Museum, and the Burger Collection, Hong Kong.

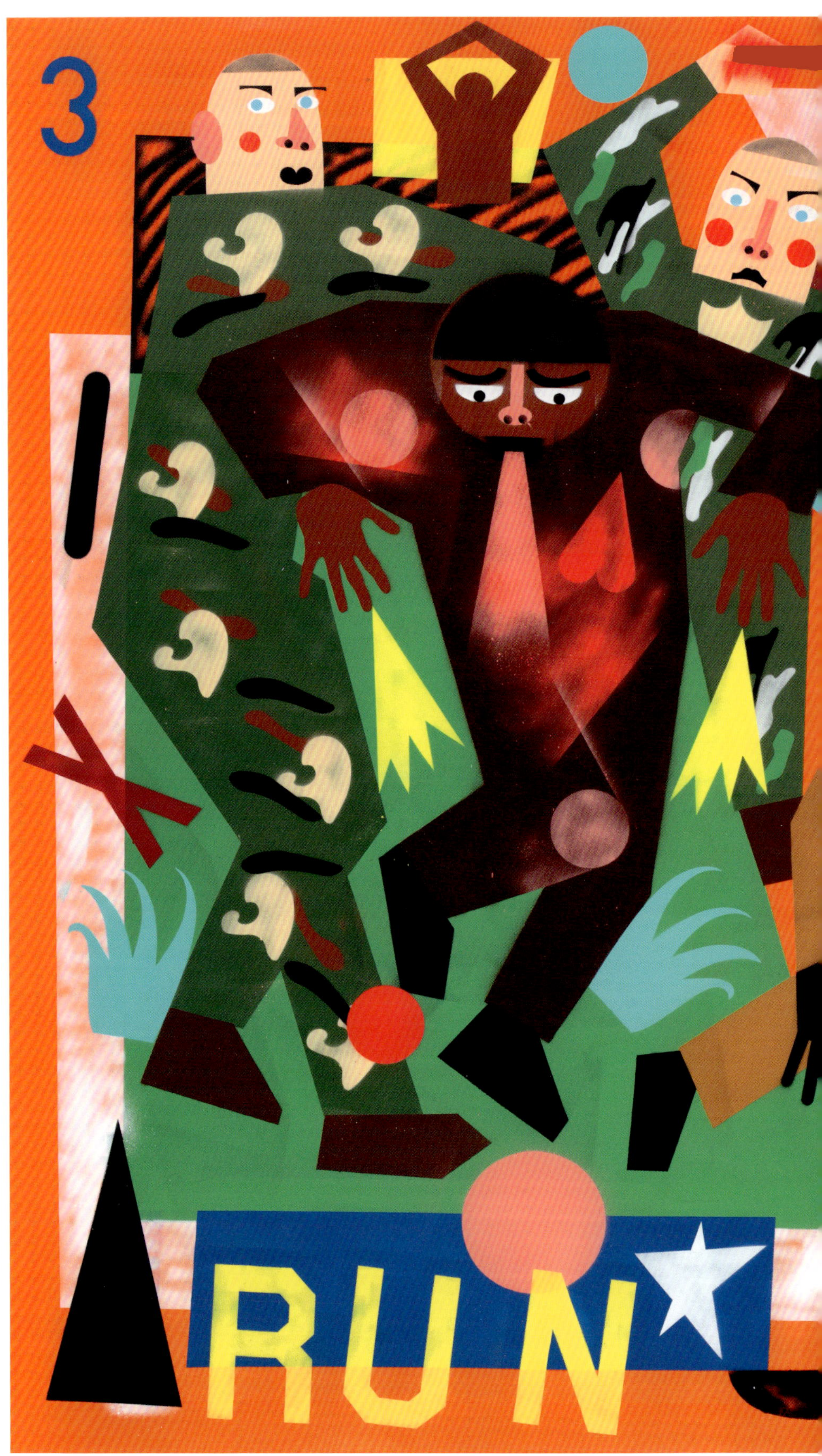

Always Ready, Always There, 2018
Acrylic and spray paint on canvas
84⅛ × 120¼ × 1¾ inches

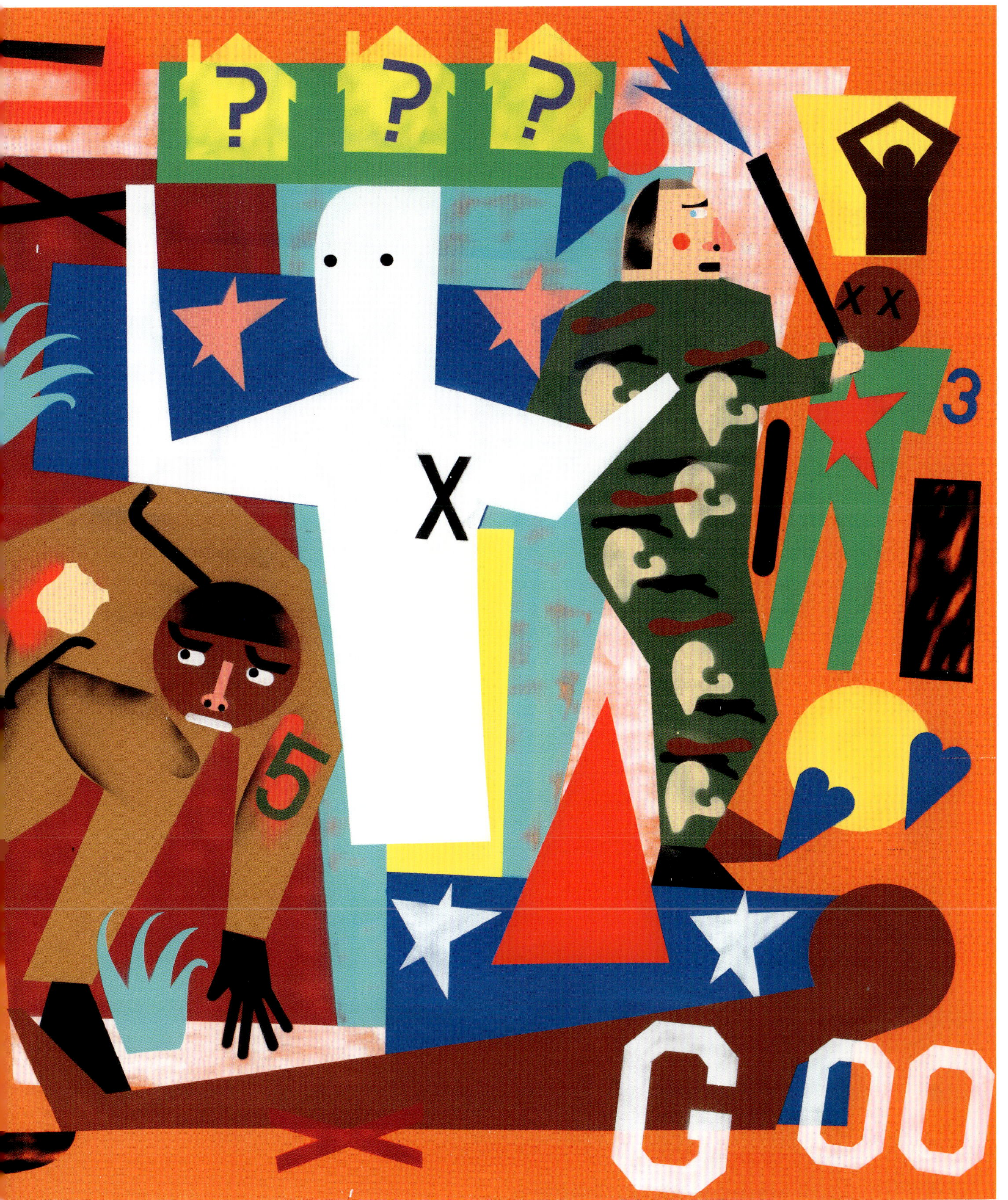

? ? ?
X
5
X X
3
G OO

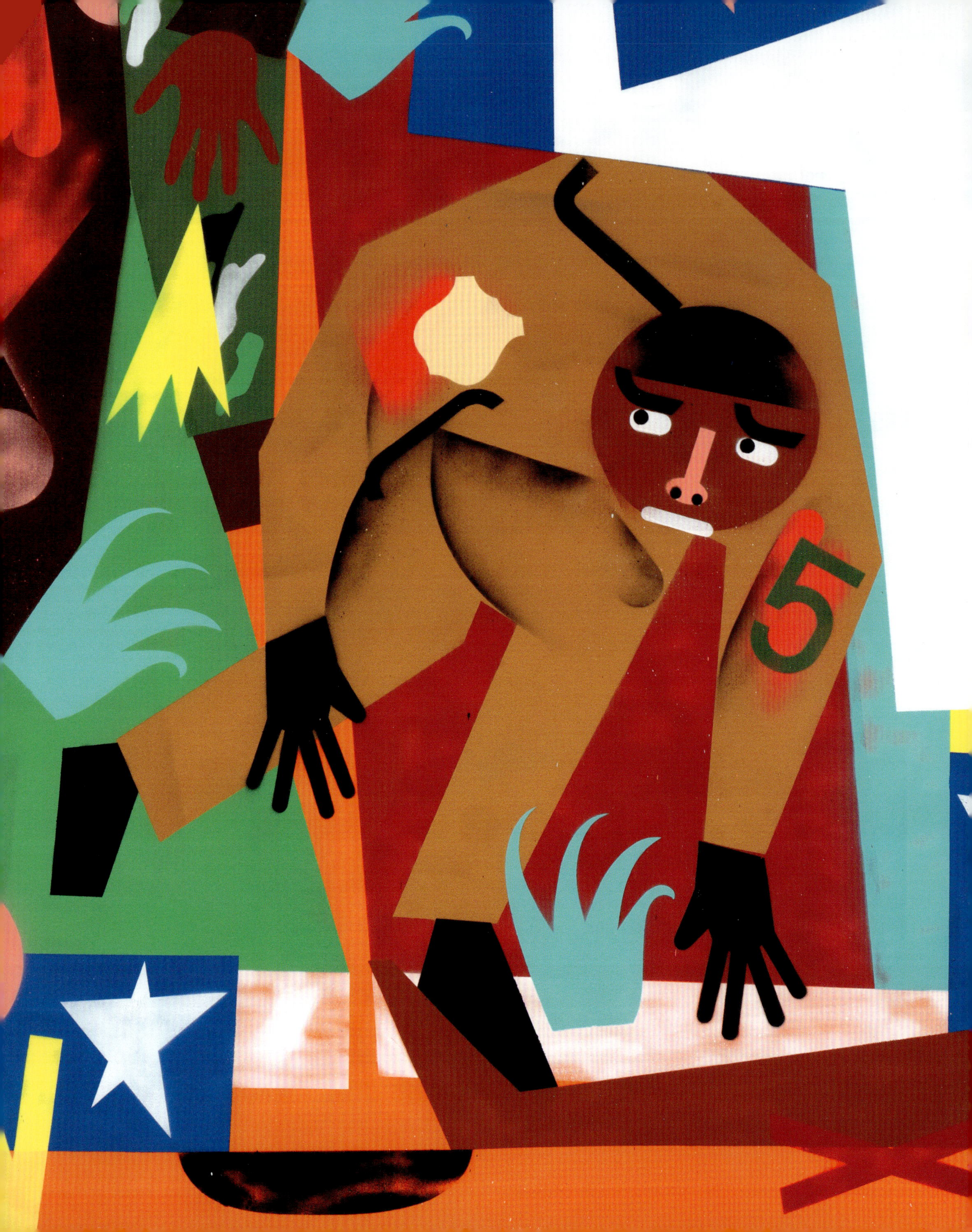

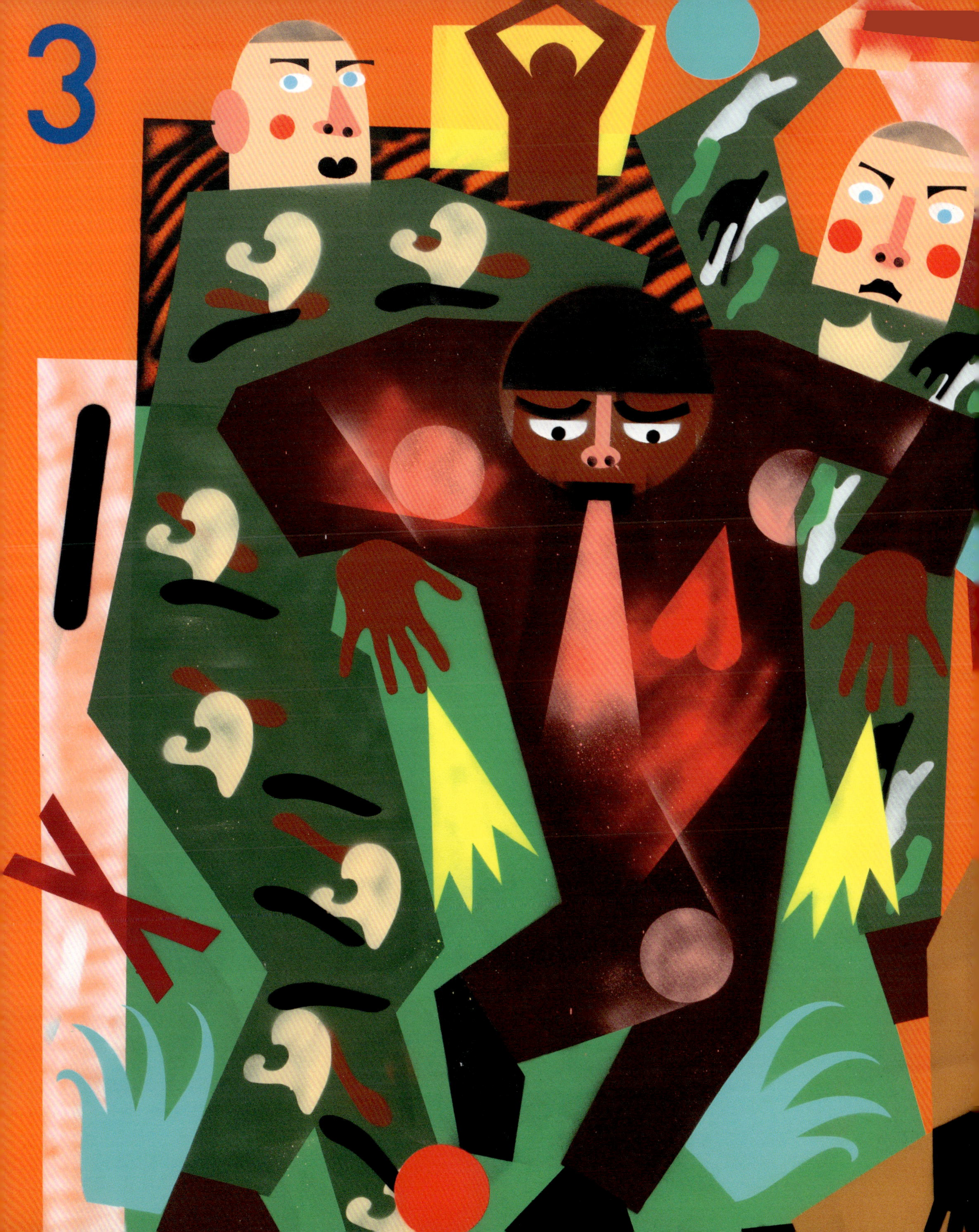
3

ruby onyinyechi
amanze

ruby onyinyechi amanze (b. 1982, Port-Harcourt, Nigeria) is a Philadelphia-based artist of Nigerian descent with a British upbringing whose creative process focuses on producing mixed media paper-based drawings and works. Her art draws inspiration from photography, textiles, architecture, and printmaking, and amanze builds her practice around questions of how to create drawings that maintain paper's essence of weightlessness. amanze's large-scaled, multidimensional drawings are part of an ongoing, yet nonlinear narrative that employs the malleability of space as the primary antagonist.

A nameless, self-imagined, chimeric universe has simultaneously been positioned between nowhere and everywhere. Using a limited palette of visual elements, including ada the Alien, windows, and birds, amanze's drawings create a non-narrative and expansive world. The construction of this world is largely centered around an interest in the spatial negotiations found in the three-dimensional practices of dance, architecture, and design.

Most recently, amanze completed two-year-long residencies at the Queens Museum and as part of the Drawing Center's Open Sessions Program, both in New York. She has exhibited her work internationally in Lagos, London, Johannesburg, and Paris, and nationally at the California African American Museum, the Drawing Center, and the Studio Museum in Harlem.

amanze earned her BFA, Summa Cum Laude, from Tyler School of Art at Temple University, and her MFA from Cranbrook Academy of Art. In 2012–13, amanze was a Fulbright Scholar at the University of Nigeria, Nsukka. Today, she resides between Philadelphia and Brooklyn but calls multiple places home.

Dive Sky, 2020
Photo transfer, graphite, ink,
metallic enamel, gouache,
acrylic on paper
59 × 67 × 2 inches

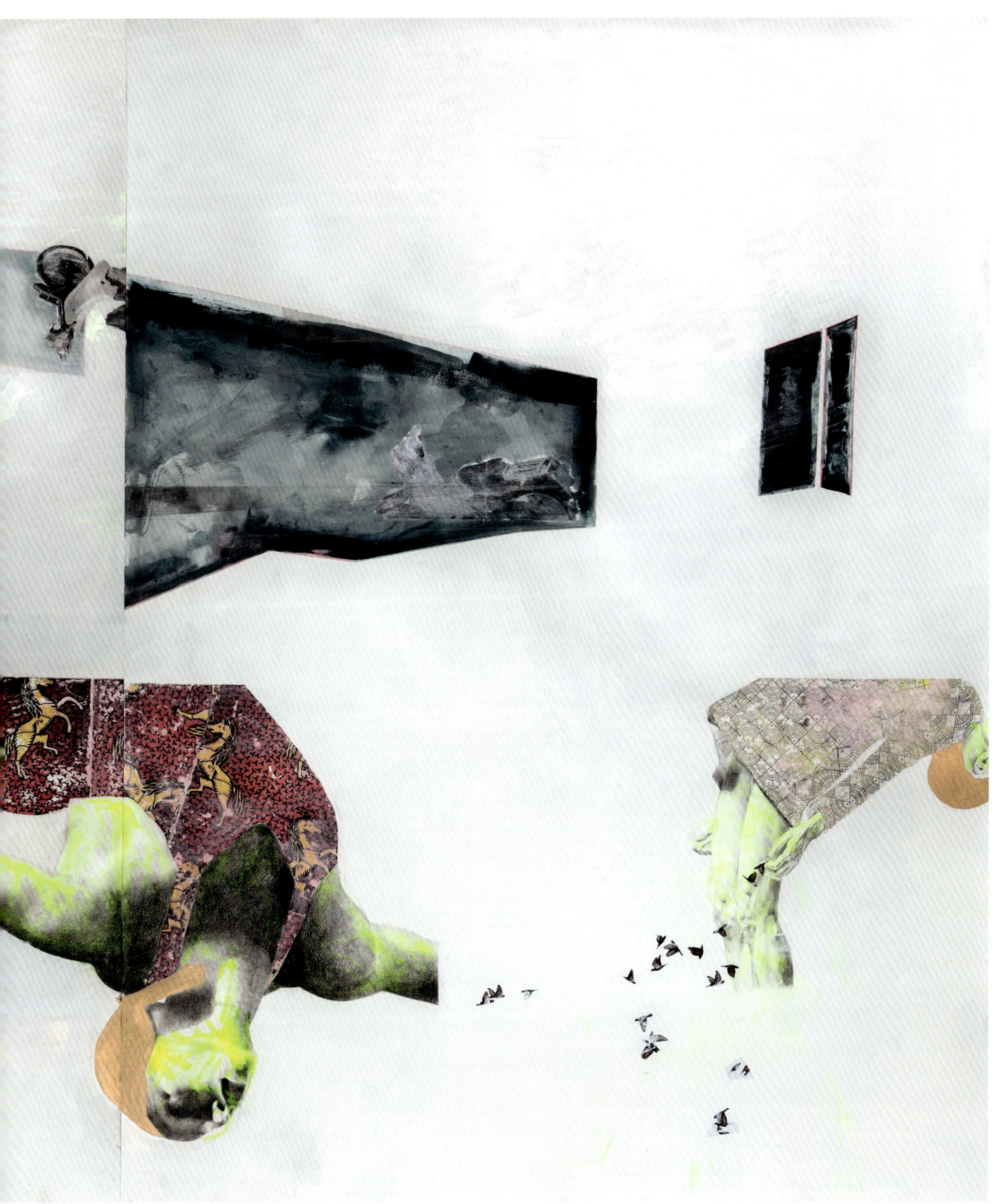

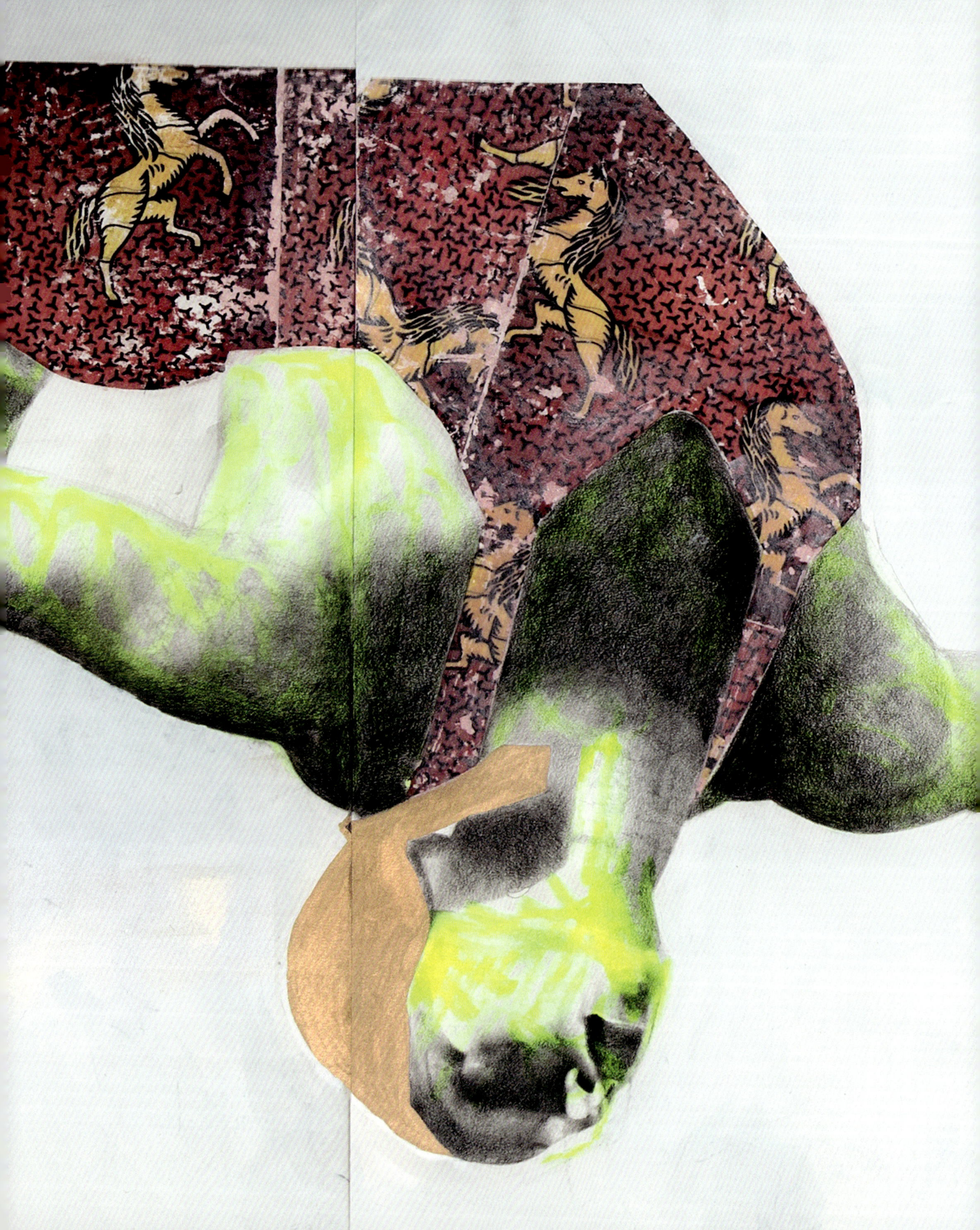

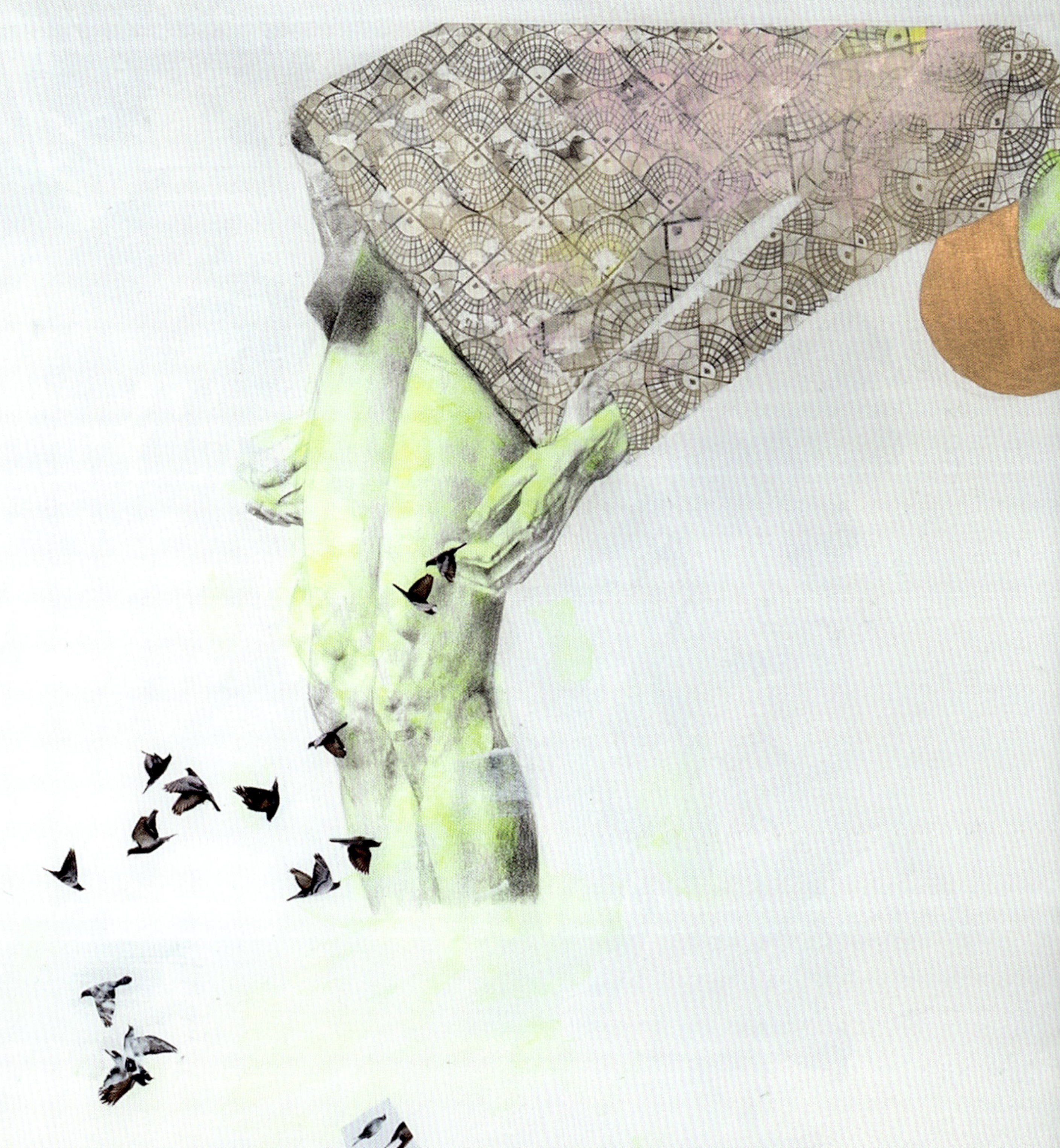

LAUREN
HALSEY

Lauren Halsey is rethinking the possibilities for art, architecture, and community engagement. She produces both standalone artworks and site-specific projects, particularly in the South Central neighborhood of Los Angeles, where her family has lived for several generations. Combining found, fabricated, and handmade objects, Halsey's work maintains a sense of civic urgency and free-flowing imagination, reflecting the lives of the people and places around her and addressing the crucial issues confronting people of color, queer populations, and the working class. Critiques of gentrification and disenfranchisement are accompanied by real-world proposals and celebration of on-the-ground aesthetics. Inspired by Afrofuturism and funk, as well as the signs and symbols that populate her local environments, Halsey creates a visionary form of culture that is at once radical and collaborative.

Halsey (b. 1987, Los Angeles, CA; lives and works in Los Angeles, CA) has been the subject of solo exhibitions at institutions including Seattle Art Museum, WA (2022); Museum of Fine Arts, Boston, MA (2021); Fondation Louis Vuitton, Paris, France (2019); and the Museum of Contemporary Art, Los Angeles, CA (2018). In 2023, Halsey was commissioned by the Metropolitan Museum of Art, New York, NY, to create a site-specific installation for its Iris and B. Gerald Cantor Roof Garden. Halsey is the 2021 recipient of Seattle Art Museum's Gwendolyn Knight | Jacob Lawrence Prize and received the Mohn Award for artistic excellence at the Hammer Museum's *Made in L.A.* 2018 biennial.

Her work is in the collections of the Museum of Modern Art, New York, NY; Institute of Contemporary Art, Miami, FL; Museum of Fine Arts, Boston, MA; Columbus Museum of Art, OH; Hammer Museum, Los Angeles, CA; and the Museum of Contemporary Art, Los Angeles, CA. In 2020, Halsey founded Summaeverythang Community Center and is currently developing a major public monument for South Central Los Angeles.

WE IN HERE, 2022
Watercolor ink, colored pencil, collage,
and hand carving on gypsum
140¾ × 23½ × 23½ inches

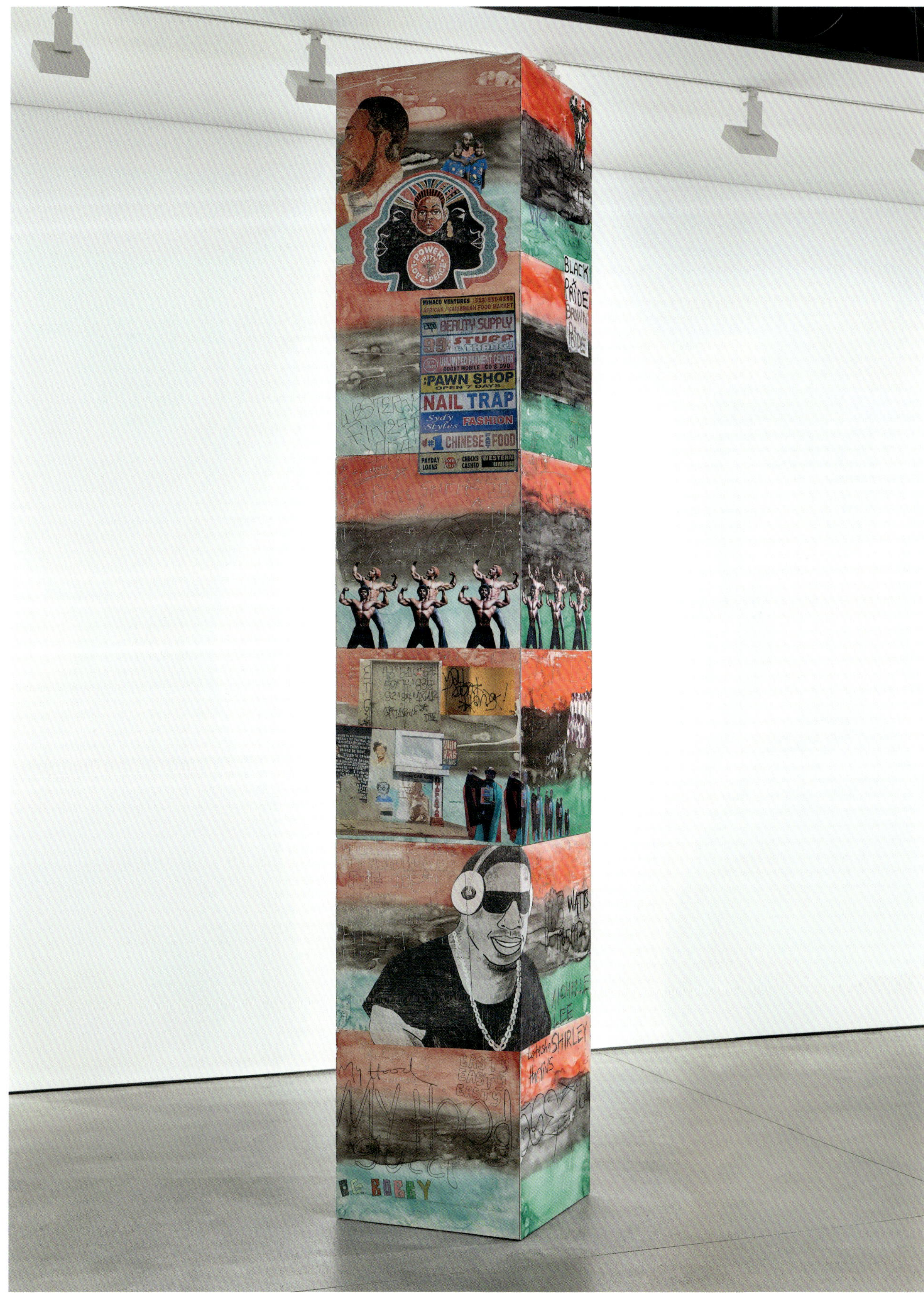

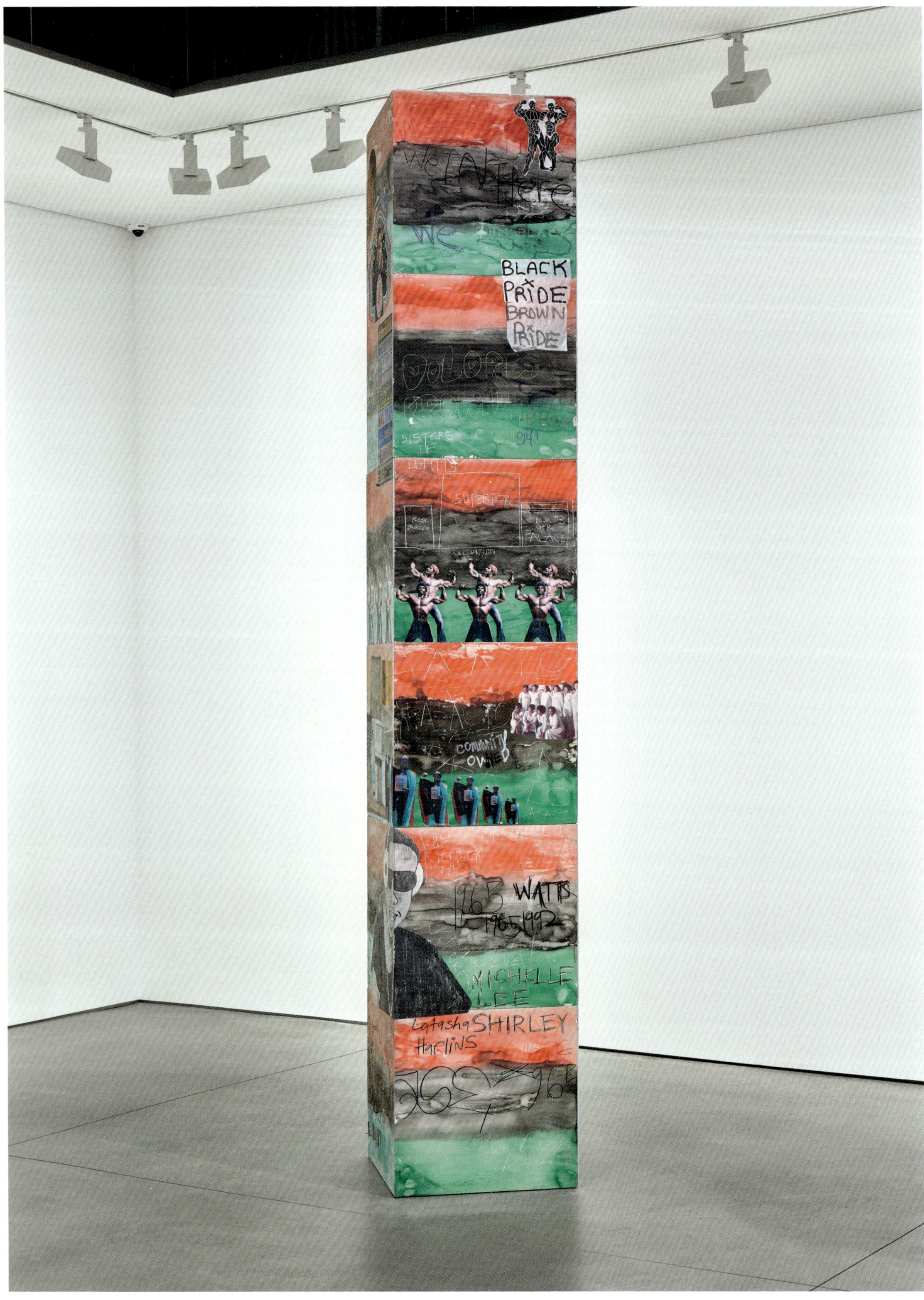

We A Here
we
BLACK PRIDE
BROWN PRIDE
SISTERS
SUPERIOR
BURGER PALACE
COMUNITY OWNED
1965 WATTS
1965 1992
MICHELLE LEE
Latasha Harlins
SHIRLEY

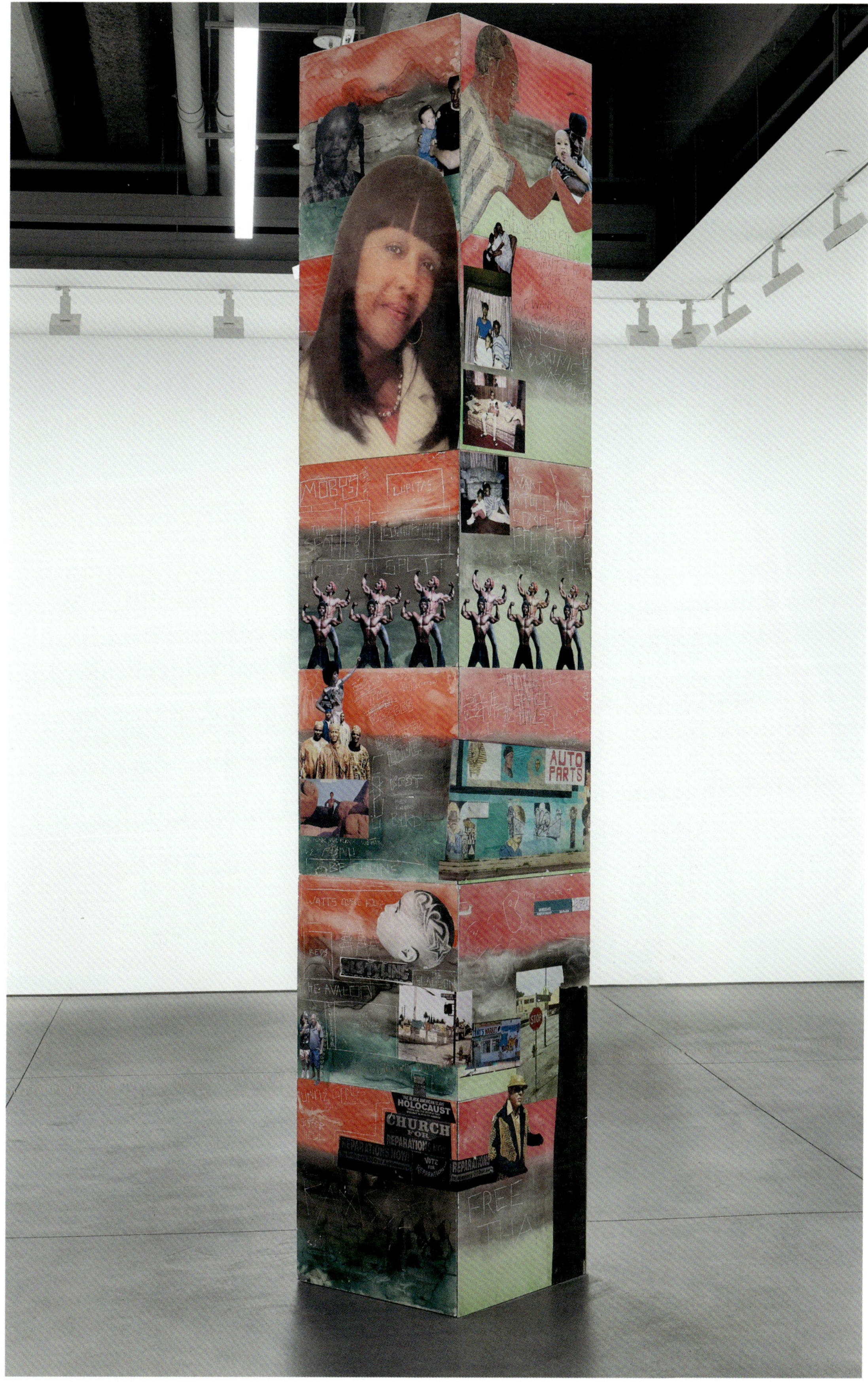

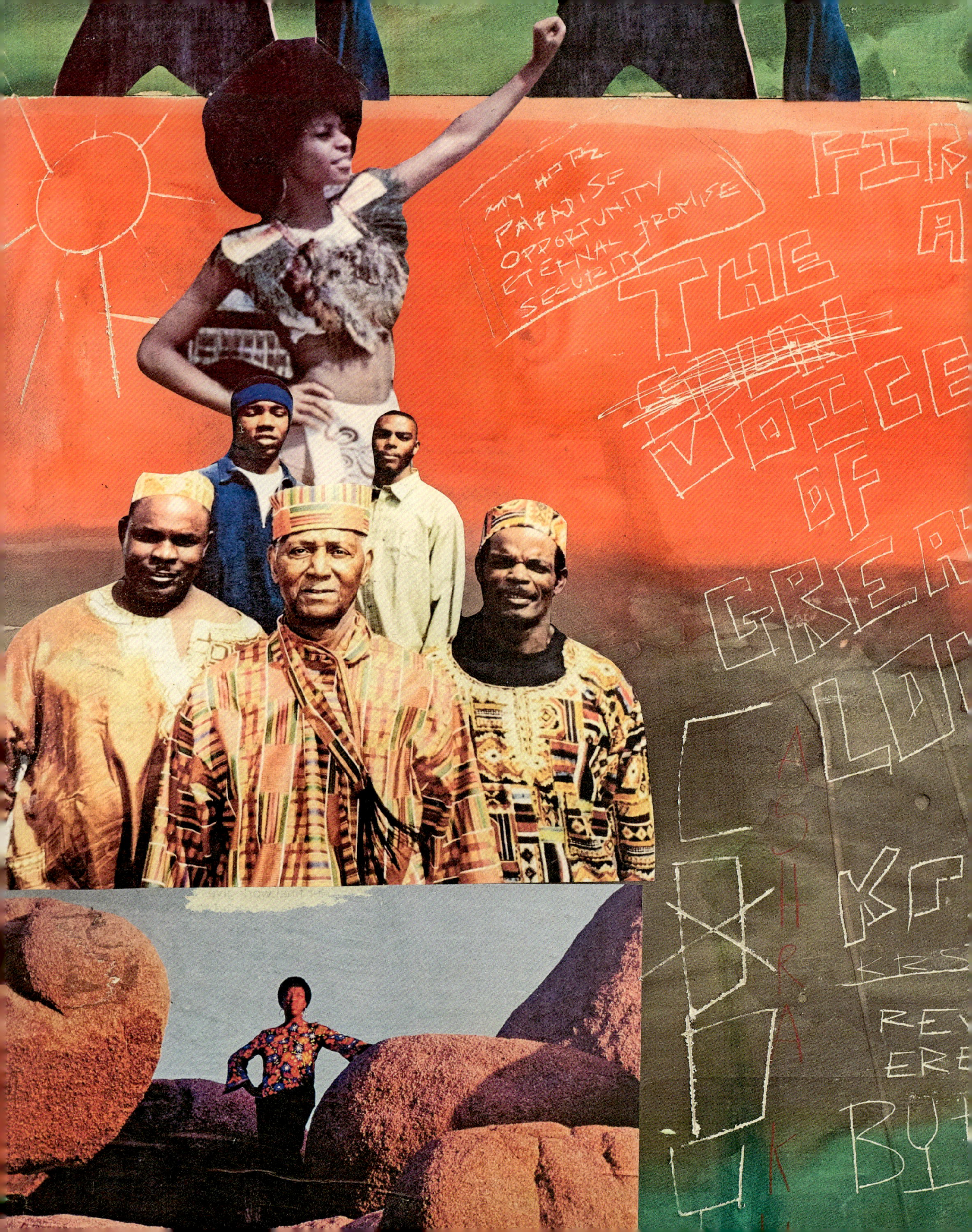

MY HOPE
PARADISE
OPPORTUNITY
ETERNAL PROMISE
SECURITY
FIR A
THE
VOICE
OF
GREAT

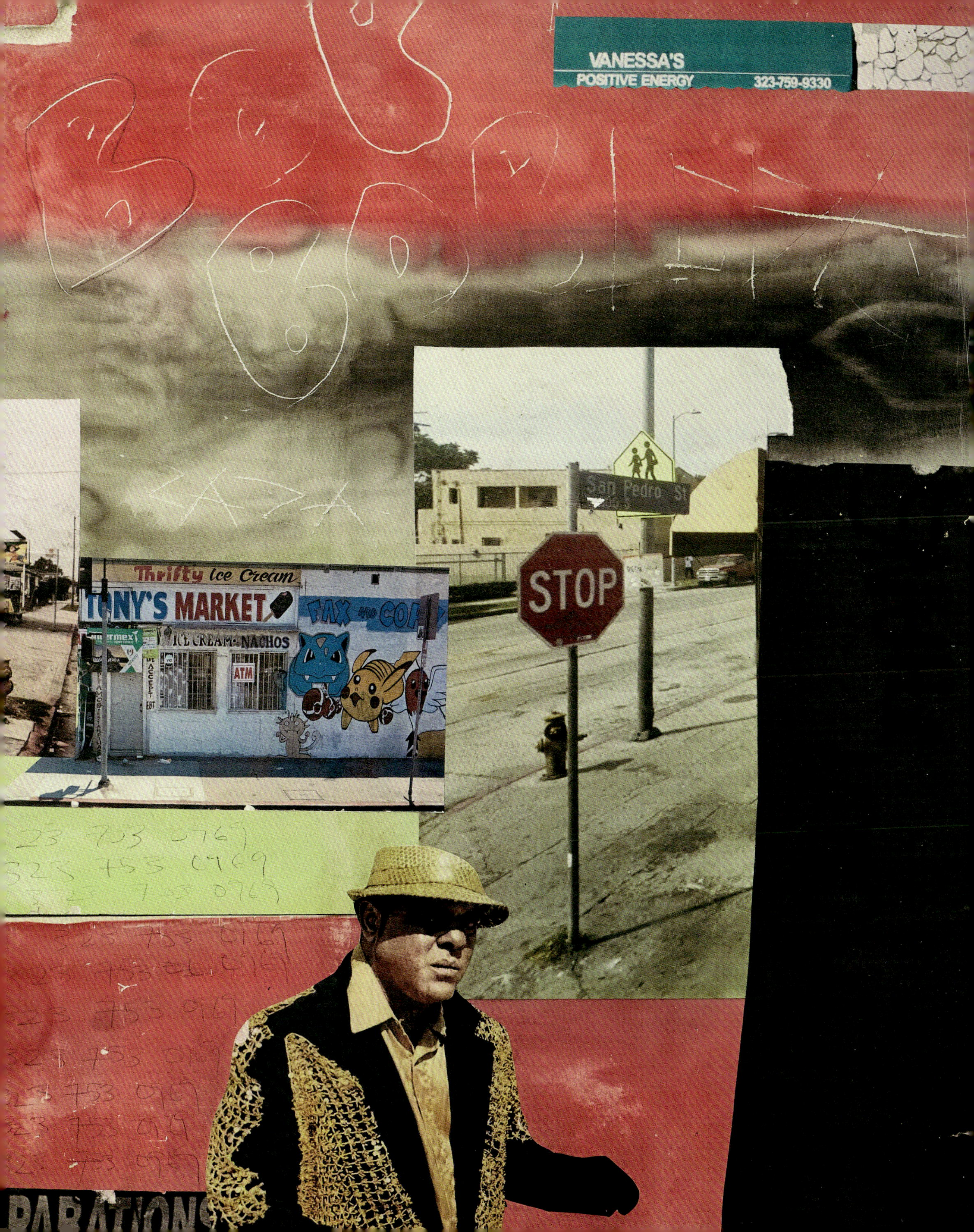

VANESSA'S
POSITIVE ENERGY
323-759-9330
San Pedro St
STOP
Thrifty Ice Cream
TONY'S MARKET
FAX AND COPY
ICE CREAM · NACHOS
ATM
WE ACCEPT EBT

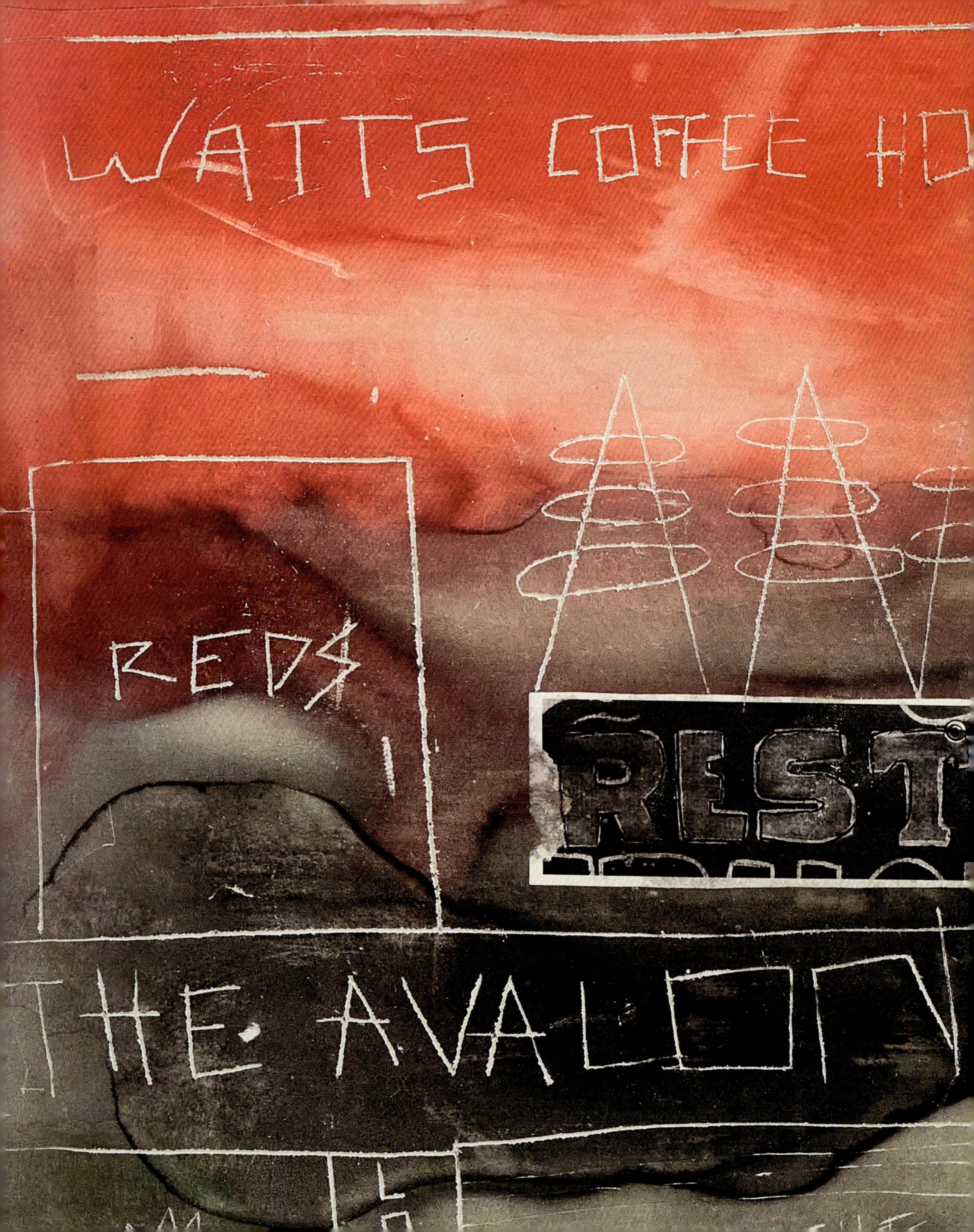

WATTS COFFEE HO
REDS
REST
THE AVALON

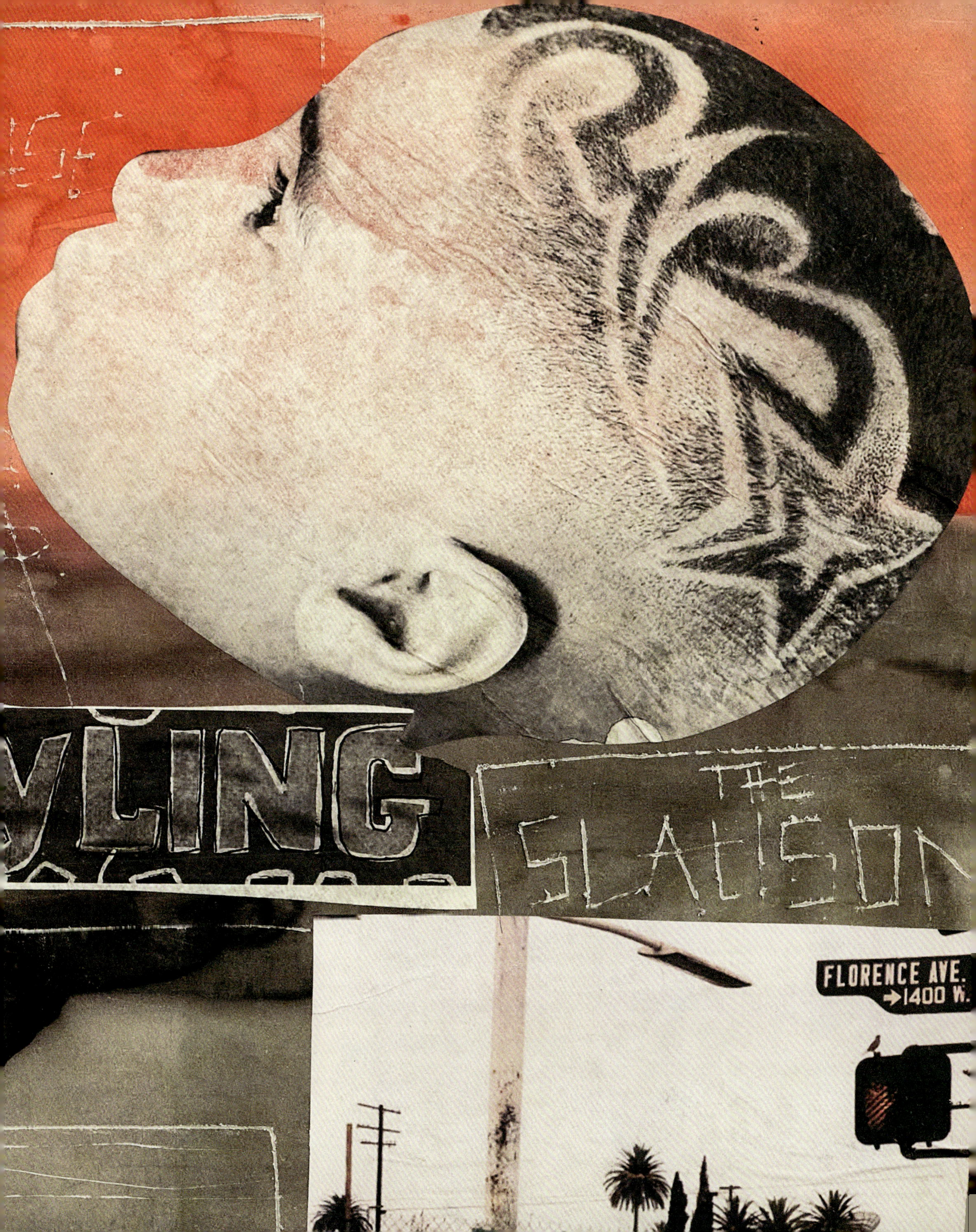

YLING
THE SLAUSON
FLORENCE AVE.
→ 1400 W.

RACHEL
JONES

Rachel Jones is an artist working in painting, installation, sound, and performance. Jones explores a sense of self as a visual, visceral experience. In her paintings, she grapples with the challenges of finding visual means to convey abstract, existential concepts. In depicting the psychological truths of being and the emotions these engender, abstraction becomes a way of expressing the intangible. The artist repeats motifs and symbols across her series to create associative, even familial, relationships between them, underscoring their kinship as part of her ongoing investigation of identity. Her expressive use of color becomes a way of provoking or communicating with viewers, who bring their own lived experiences and cultural backgrounds to the interpretation of her works. This sense of community and shared history comes to the fore in her installations and performances, in which imagery, sound, and music coalesce in a celebration of Black culture.

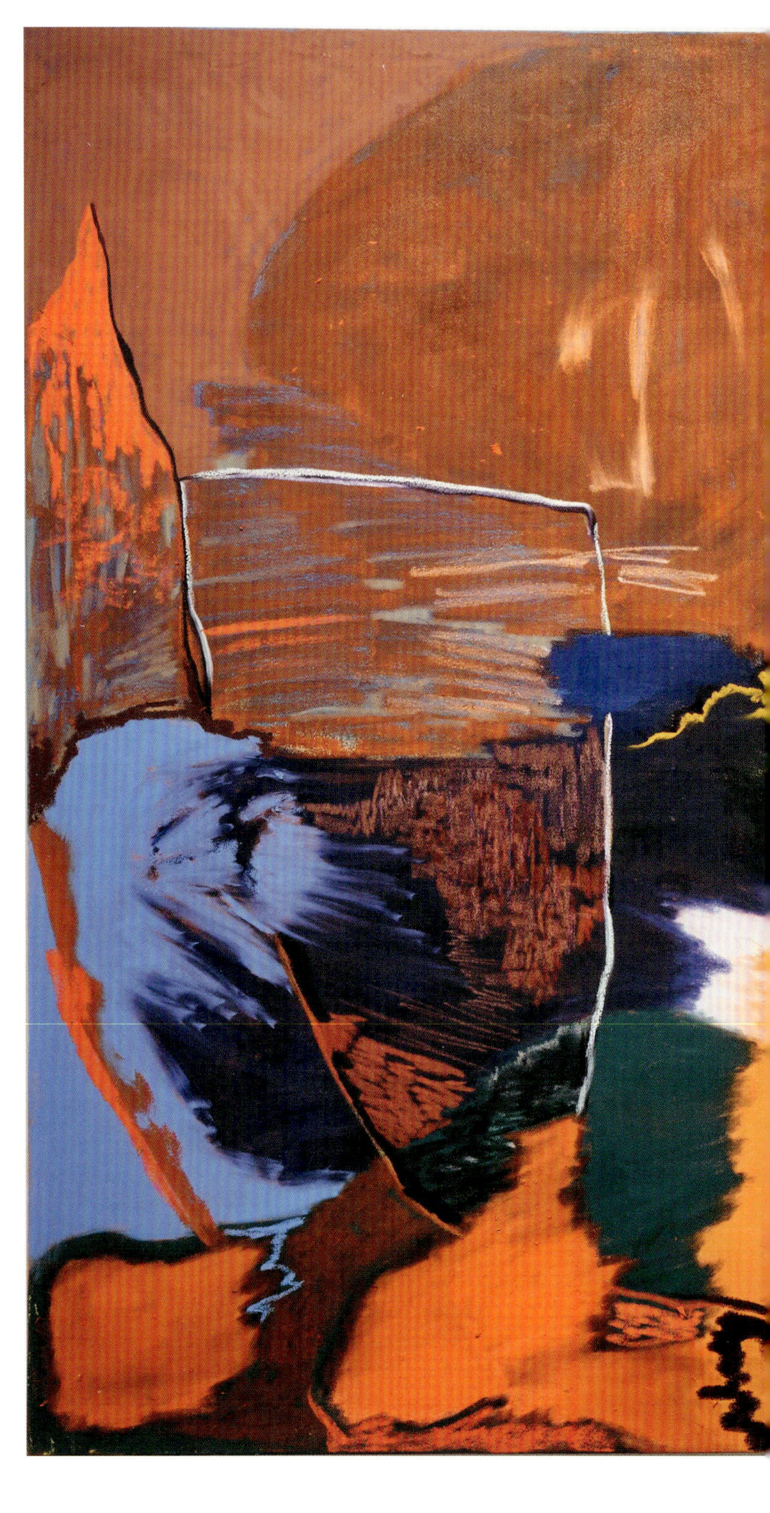

SMIIILLLLEEEE, 2021
Oil pastel and oil stick on canvas
63 × 98½ inches

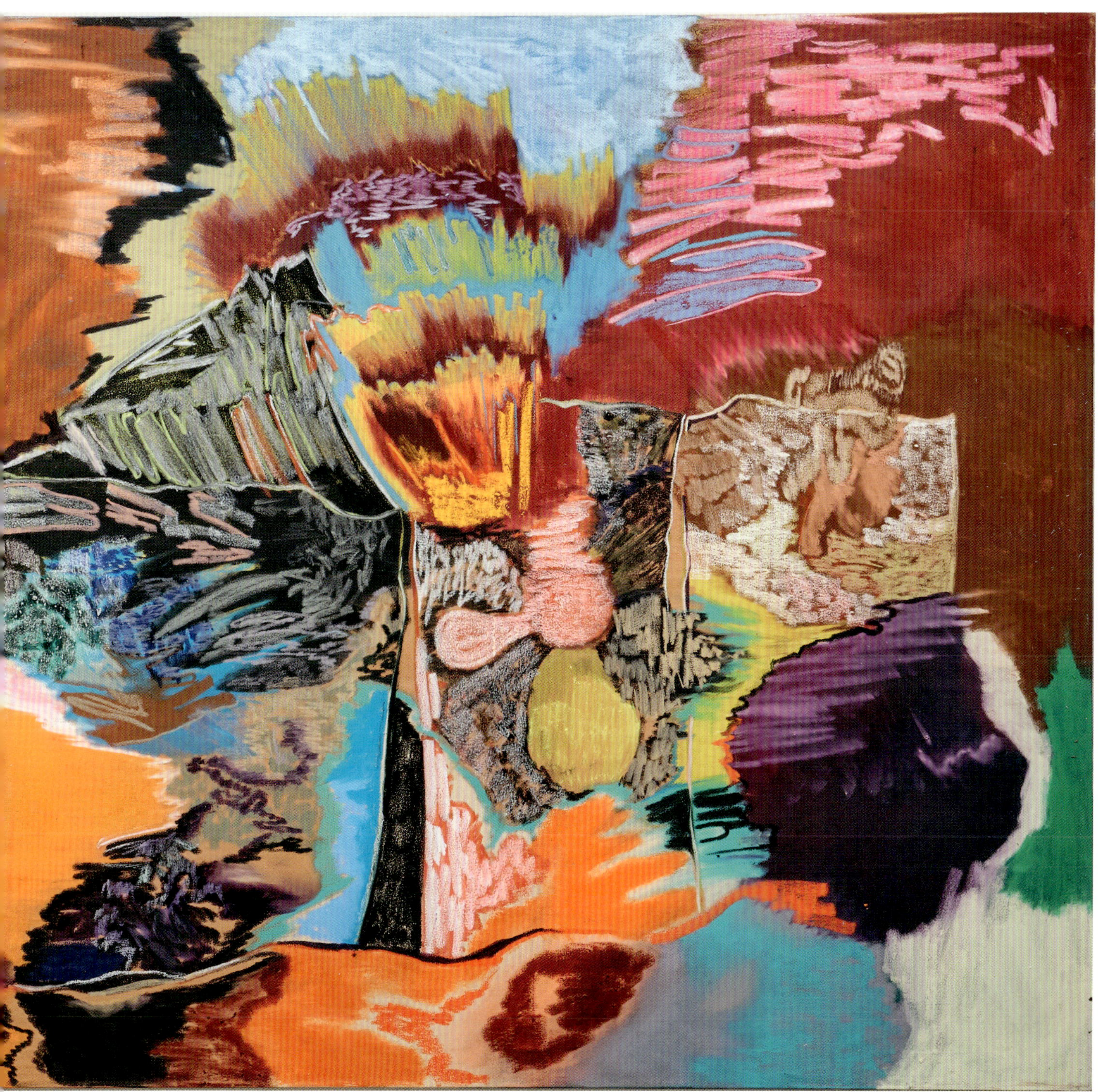

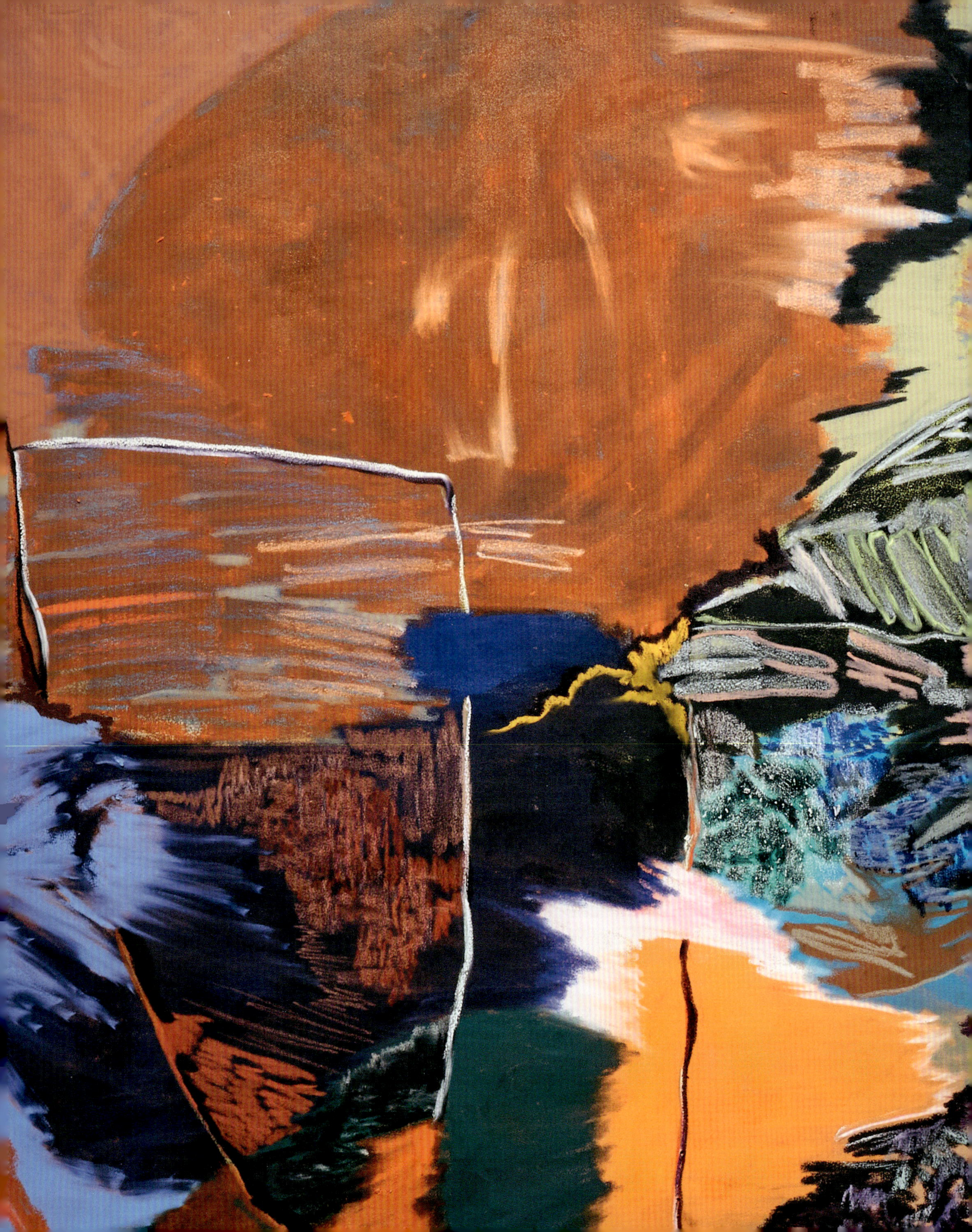

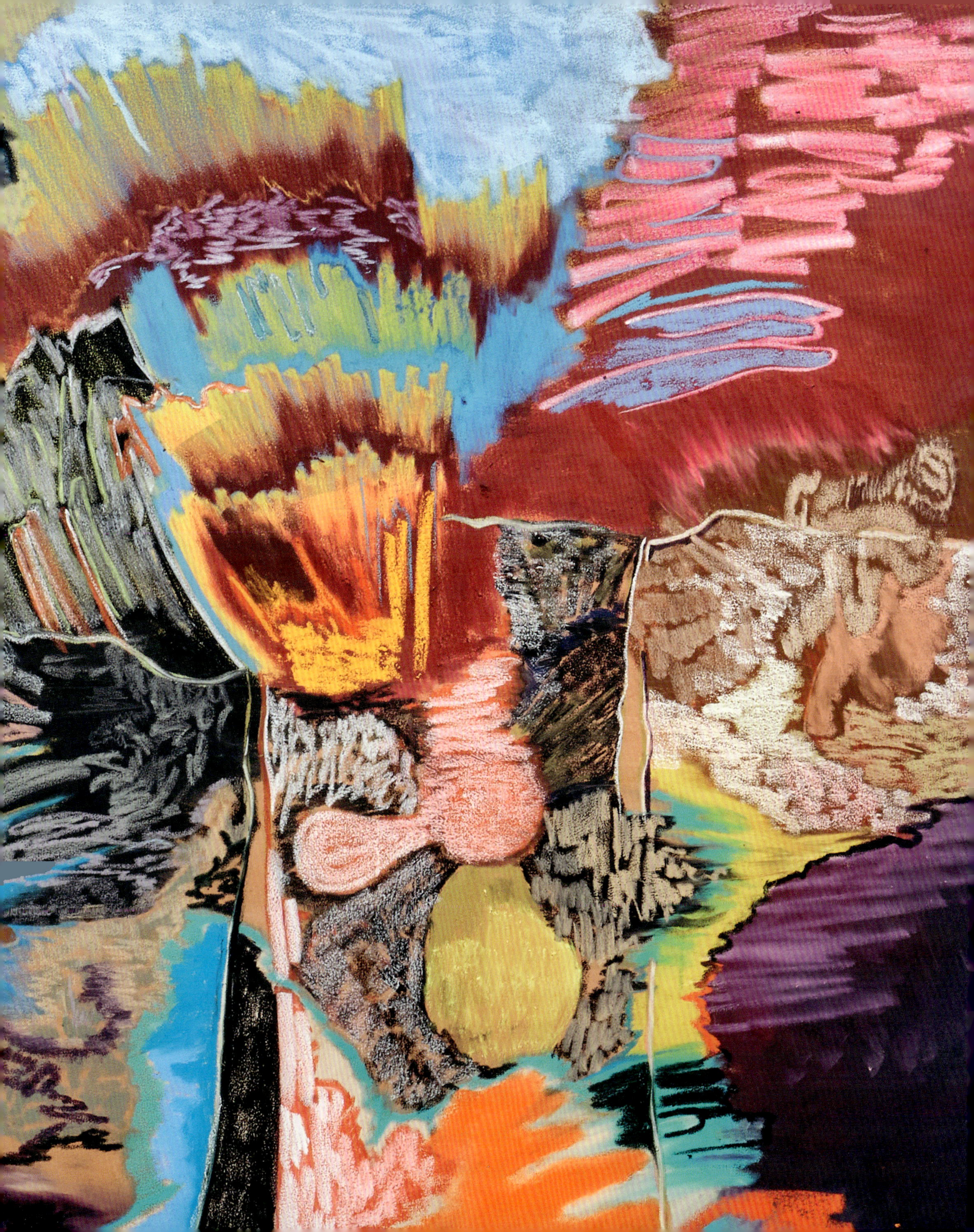

TOYIN OJIH ODUTOLA

Toyin Ojih Odutola (b. 1985, Ile-Ife, Nigeria; lives and works in New York, NY) is best known for her multimedia drawings and works on paper, which explore the malleability of identity and the possibilities in visual storytelling. Interested in the topography of skin, Ojih Odutola has a distinctive style of mark-making using only basic drawing materials, such as ballpoint pens, pencils, pastels, and charcoal. Her signature technique involves building up layers on the page through blending and shading with the highest level of detail, creating compositions that reinvent and reinterpret the traditions of portraiture. Ojih Odutola credits the development of her style to using pen, which holds a special significance through its function as a writing tool, as her work is also akin to fiction. She often spends months crafting narratives that unfold through series of artworks like the chapters of a book.

Her work is inspired by art history, popular culture, as well as her own personal history—being born in Nigeria then moving as a child to the US, where she was raised in conservative Alabama. The idea of traveling or transporting the self is a recurring theme in her work, and for Ojih Odutola, the construction of her figures is a means of discovering an individual's character and personal story. Though the representation of skin has been a core focus of her practice, she has also explored depictions of landscapes, architecture, and domestic interiors in more recent series.

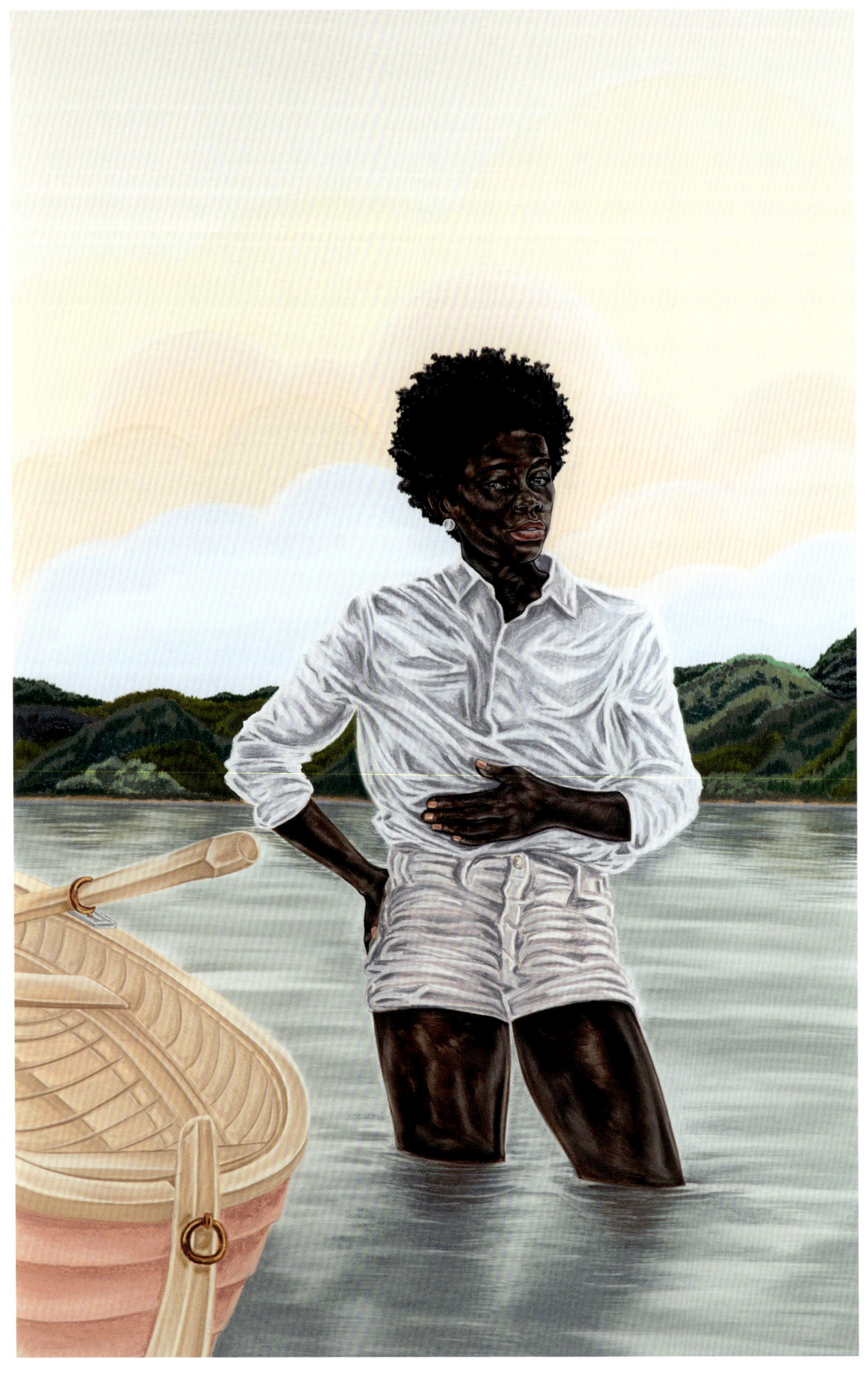

By Her Design, 2017
Charcoal, pastel, and pencil on paper
68 × 42 inches

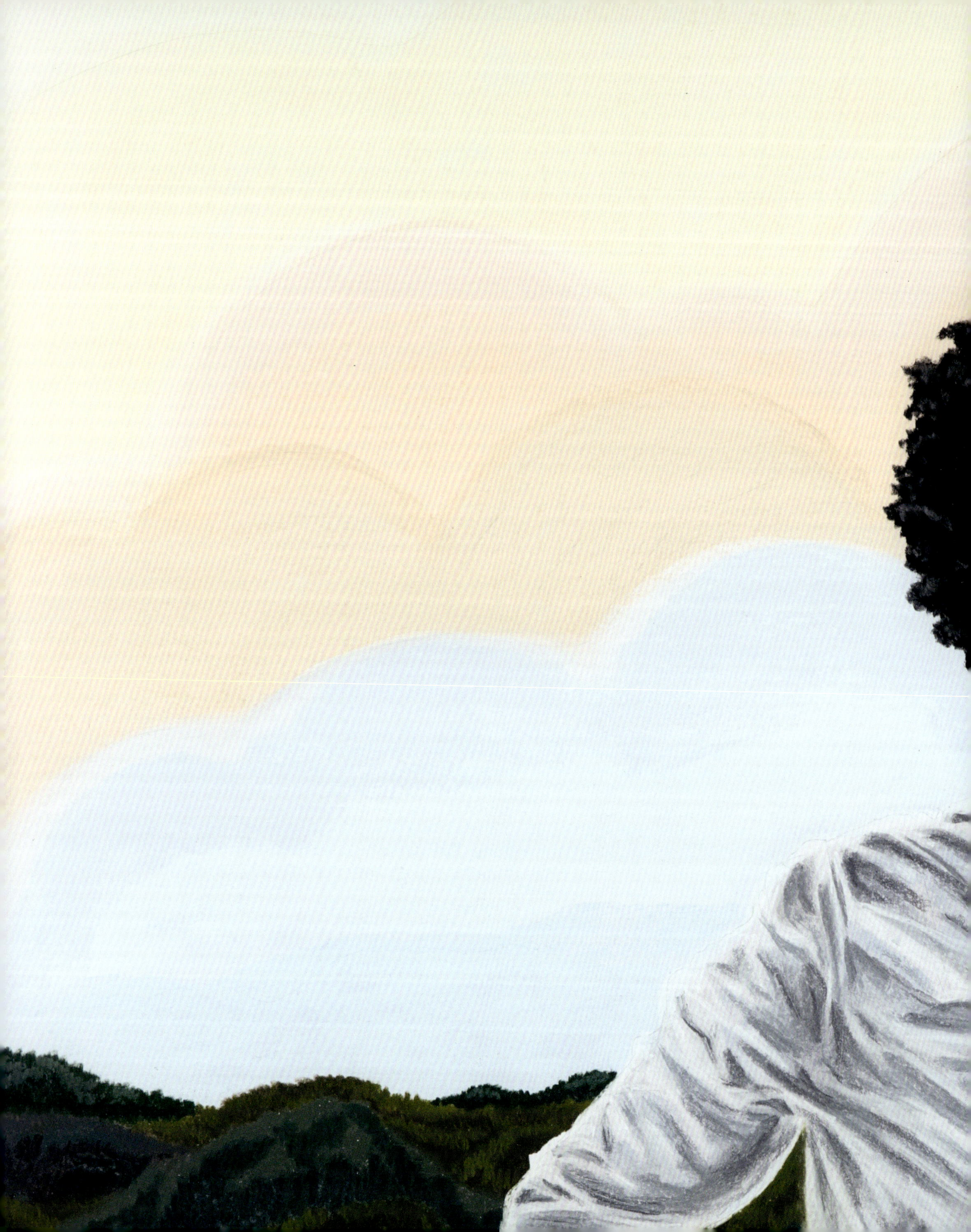

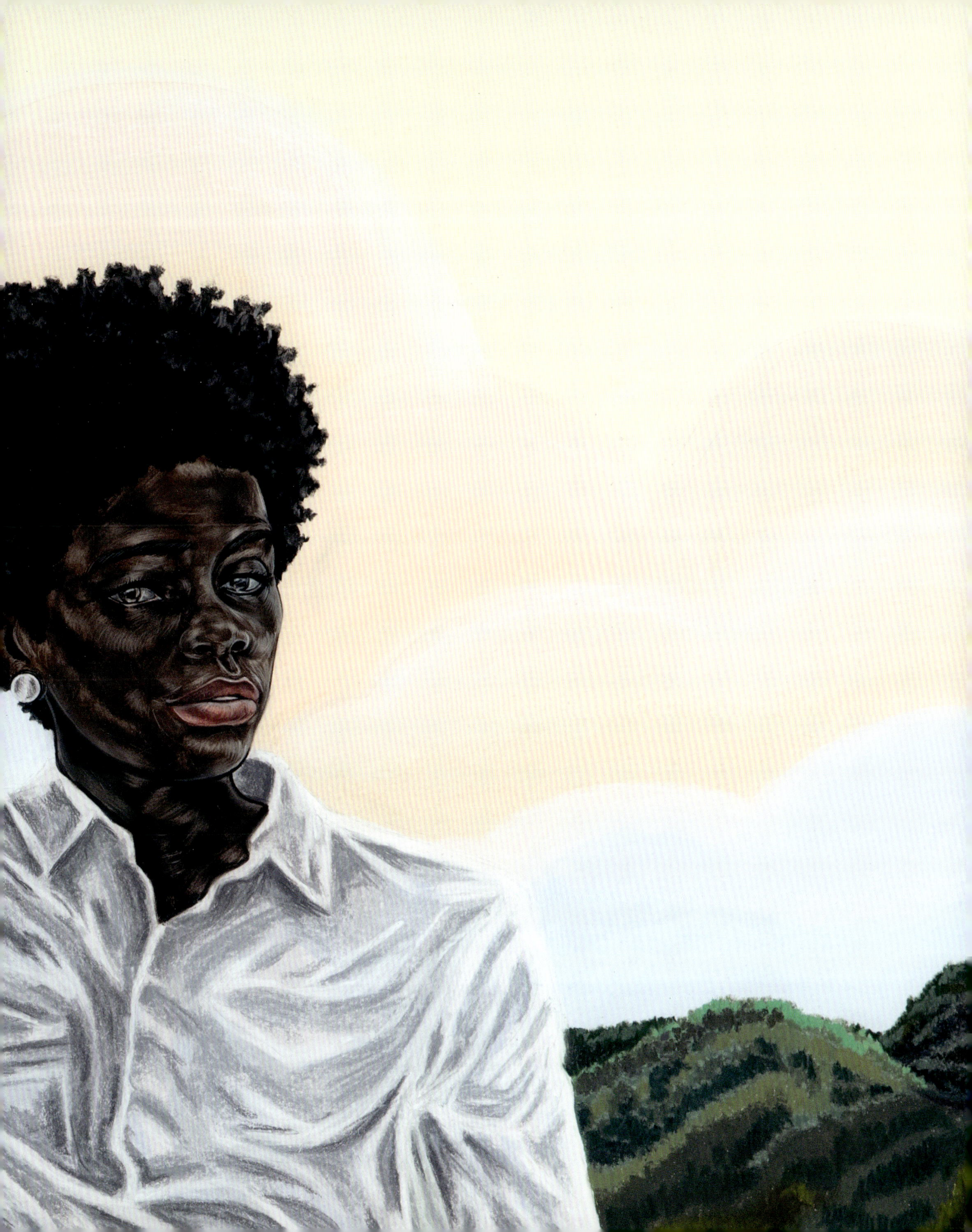

JENNIFER
PACKER

Jennifer Packer creates portraits, interior scenes, and still lifes that suggest a casual intimacy. Packer views her works as the result of an authentic encounter and exchange, and the models for her portraits – commonly friends or family members – are relaxed and seemingly unaware of the artist's or viewer's gaze. The artist's paintings are rendered in loose lines and brushstrokes using a limited color palette, often to the extent that her subject merges with or retreats into the background. Suggesting an emotional and psychological depth, her work is enigmatic, avoiding a straightforward reading: "I think about images that resist, that attempt to retain their secrets or maintain their composure, that put you to work," she explains. "I hope to make works that suggest how dynamic and complex our lives and relationships really are."

Packer (b. 1984, Philadelphia, PA; lives and works in New York, NY) received her BFA from Tyler School of Art at Temple University in 2007 and her MFA from Yale School of Art in 2012. She was the 2012–13 Artist-in-Residence at the Studio Museum in Harlem, NY, and a Visual Arts Fellow at the Fine Arts Work Center in Provincetown, MA, from 2014–16. Her work was most recently featured in two major solo exhibitions: *Jennifer Packer: The Eye Is Not Satisfied With Seeing*, presented at Serpentine Galleries, London, UK (2020), and the Whitney Museum of American Art, New York, NY (2021–22); and *Jennifer Packer: Every Shut Eye Ain't Sleep* at the Museum of Contemporary Art, Los Angeles, CA (2021–22). Her first solo institutional exhibition, *Tenderheaded*, was shown at the Renaissance Society, Chicago, IL (2017), and the Rose Art Museum, Brandeis University, Waltham, MA (2018). Her work was included in the 2019 Whitney Biennial and P.5 Prospect New Orleans (2021).

Soft Shoe, 2018
Oil on canvas
79¼ × 36 inches

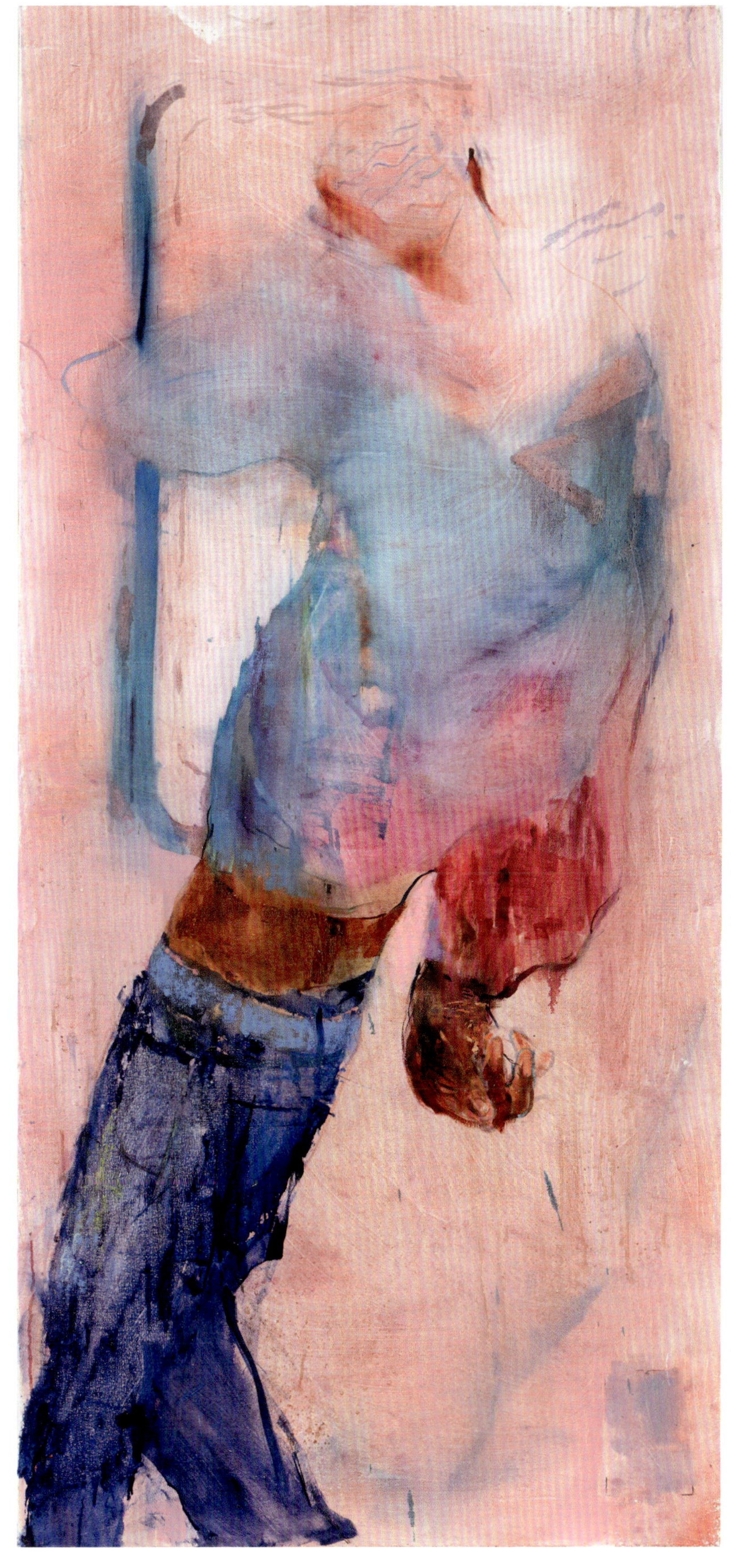

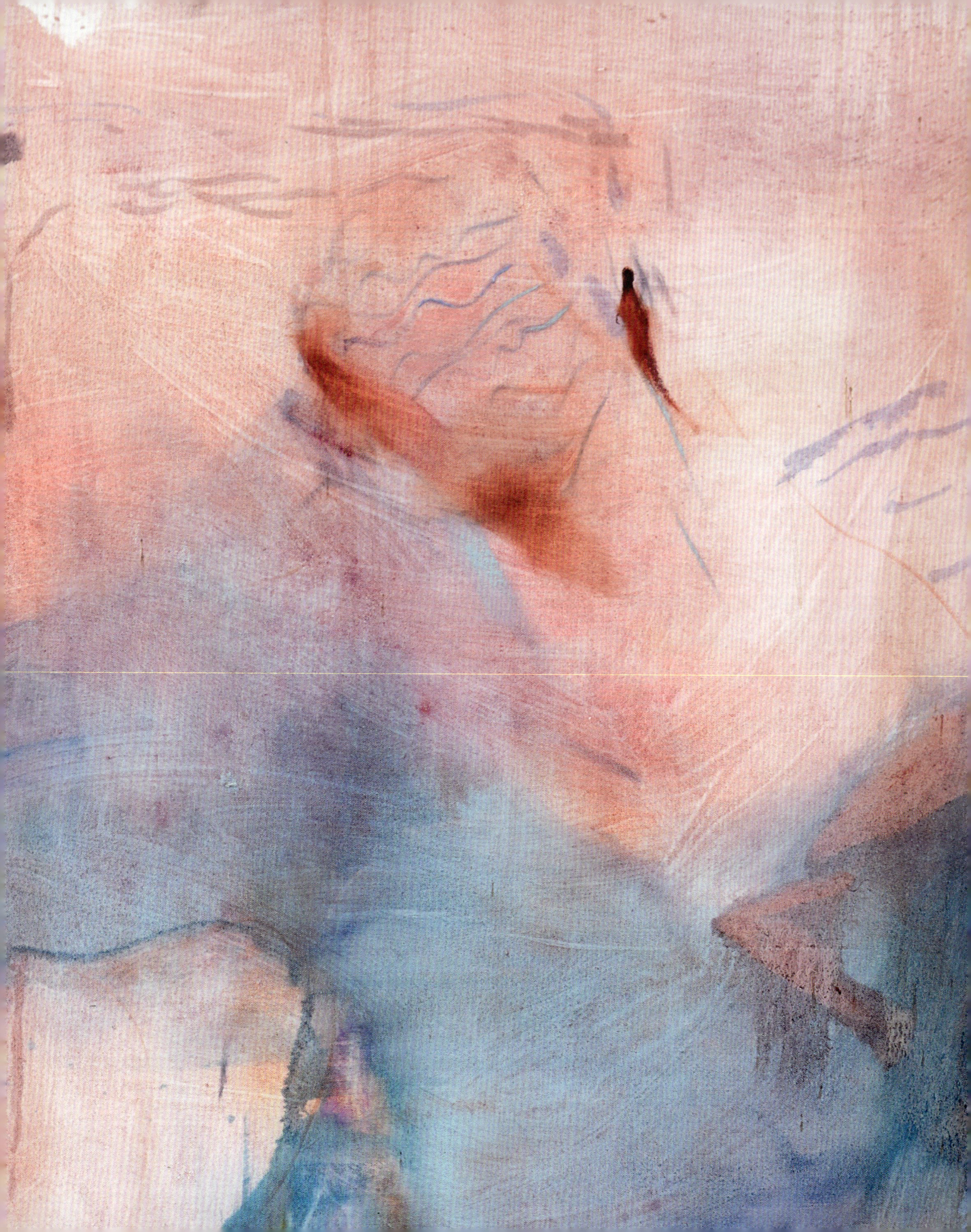

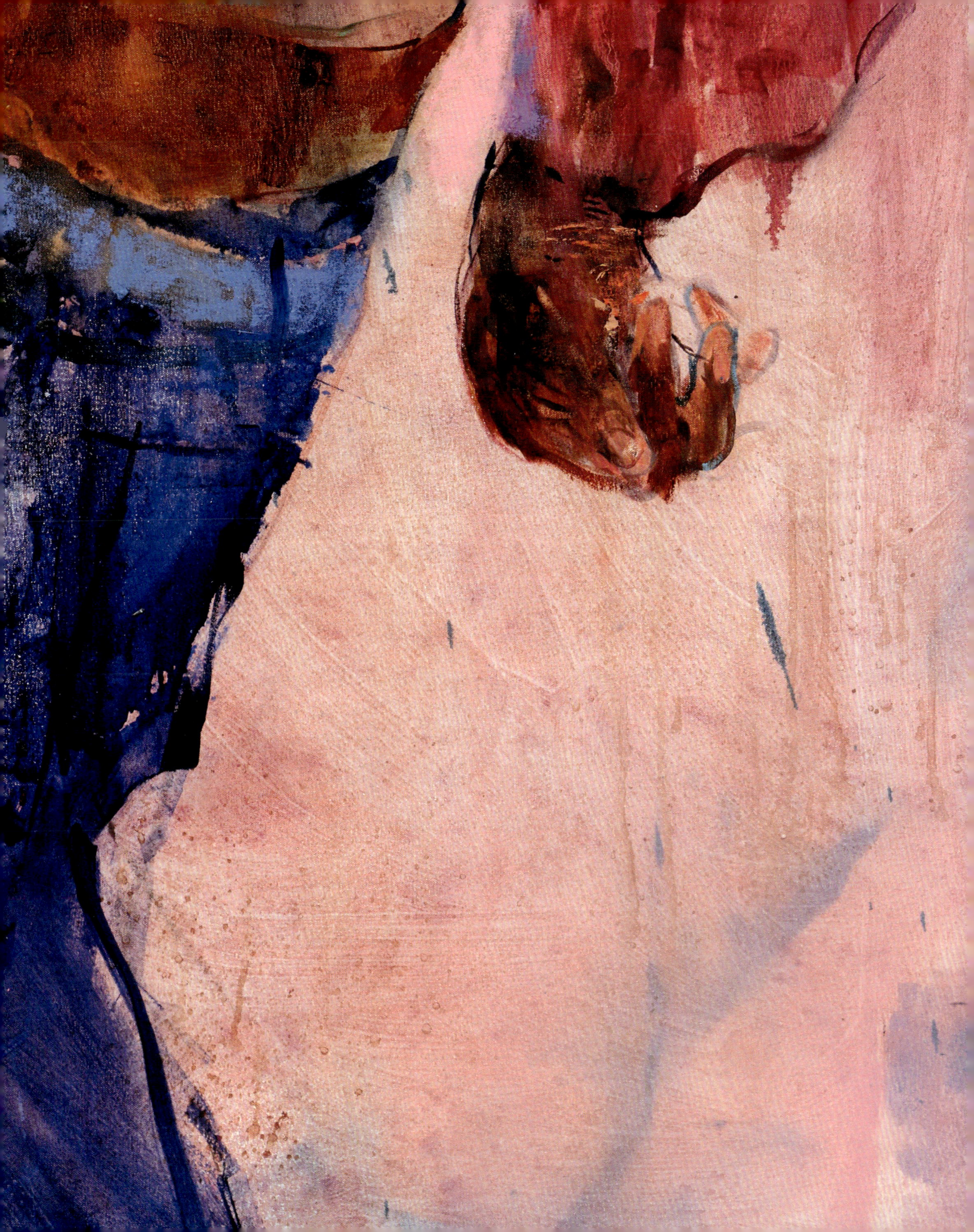

CALIDA
RAWLES

The paintings of Calida Rawles merge hyperrealism with poetic abstraction. Situating her subjects in dynamic spaces, Rawles has created recent work that employs water as a vital, organic, multifaceted material and historically charged space. Ranging from buoyant and ebullient to submerged and mysterious, Black bodies float in exquisitely rendered submarine landscapes of bubbles, ripples, refracted light, and expanses of blue. For Rawles, water signifies both physical and spiritual healing, as well as historical trauma and racial exclusion. She uses this complicated duality as a means to envision a new space for Black healing and reimagine her subjects beyond racialized tropes. Rawles' canvases represent an expansive vision of strength and tranquility during today's turbulent times while insisting on the triumph of humanity.

Rawles (b. 1976, Wilmington, DE; lives and works in Los Angeles, CA) received her BA from Spelman College, Atlanta, GA (1998), and her MA from New York University, NY (2000). Solo exhibitions of her work have been organized at Lehmann Maupin, New York, NY (2023; 2021); Various Small Fires, Los Angeles, CA (2020); and Standard Vision, Los Angeles, CA (2020). Her work has been featured in numerous group exhibitions, including: *Generation*: Jugend trotz(t) Krise*, Kunsthalle Bremen, Germany (2023); *Rose in the Concrete*, San Francisco Museum of Modern Art, CA (2023); the 12th Berlin Biennale for Contemporary Art, Germany (2022); and *Black American Portraits*, Los Angeles County Museum of Art, CA (2021), and Spelman College Museum of Fine Art, Atlanta, GA (2023). Rawles created the cover art for Ta-Nehisi Coates' debut novel, *The Water Dancer*, and her work is in numerous public and private collections, including: Dallas Museum of Art, TX; Los Angeles County Museum of Art, CA; Pérez Art Museum Miami, FL; Spelman College Museum of Fine Art, Atlanta, GA; and the Studio Museum in Harlem, NY.

Requiem for my Navigator, 2021
Acrylic on canvas
96 × 72 × 2½ inches

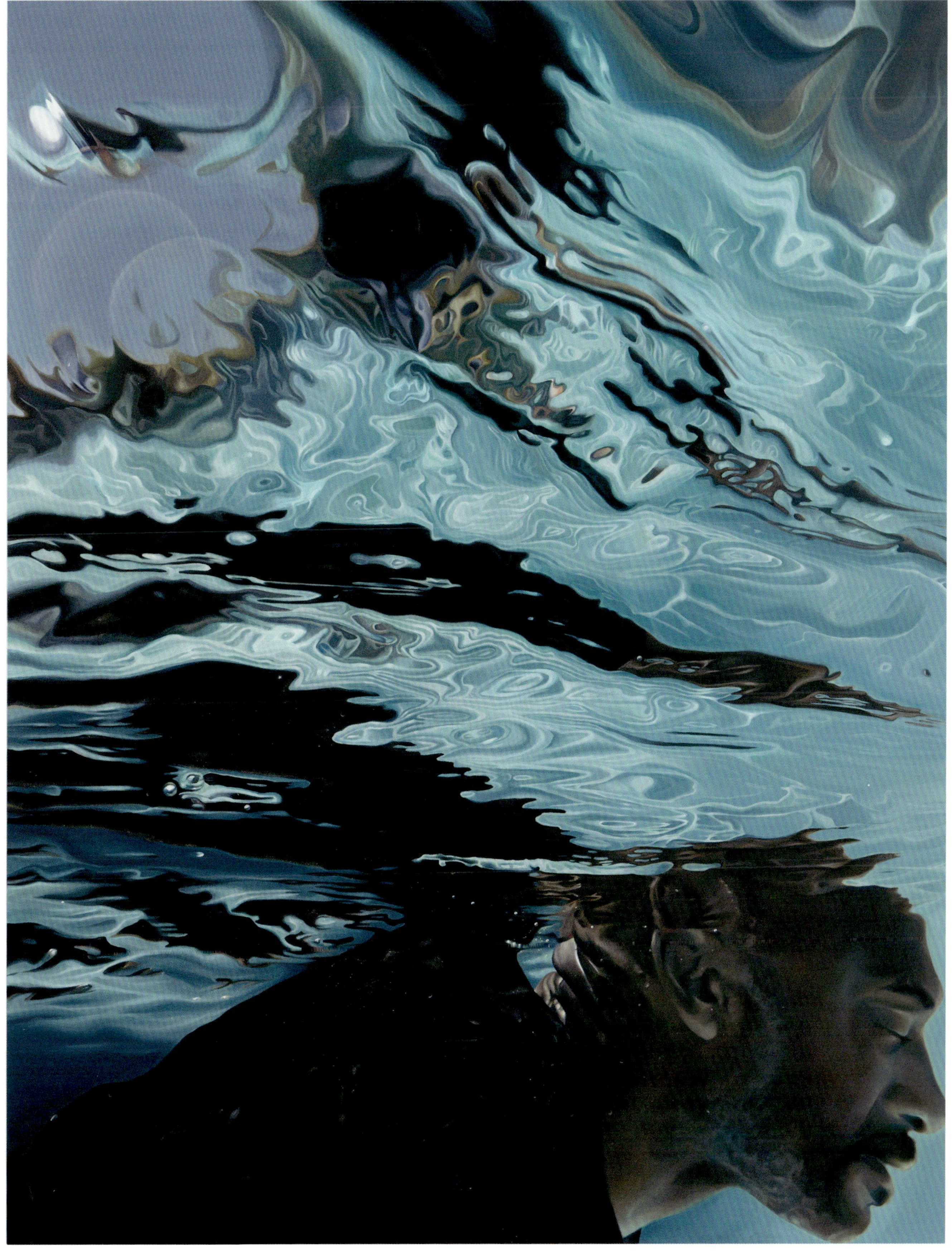

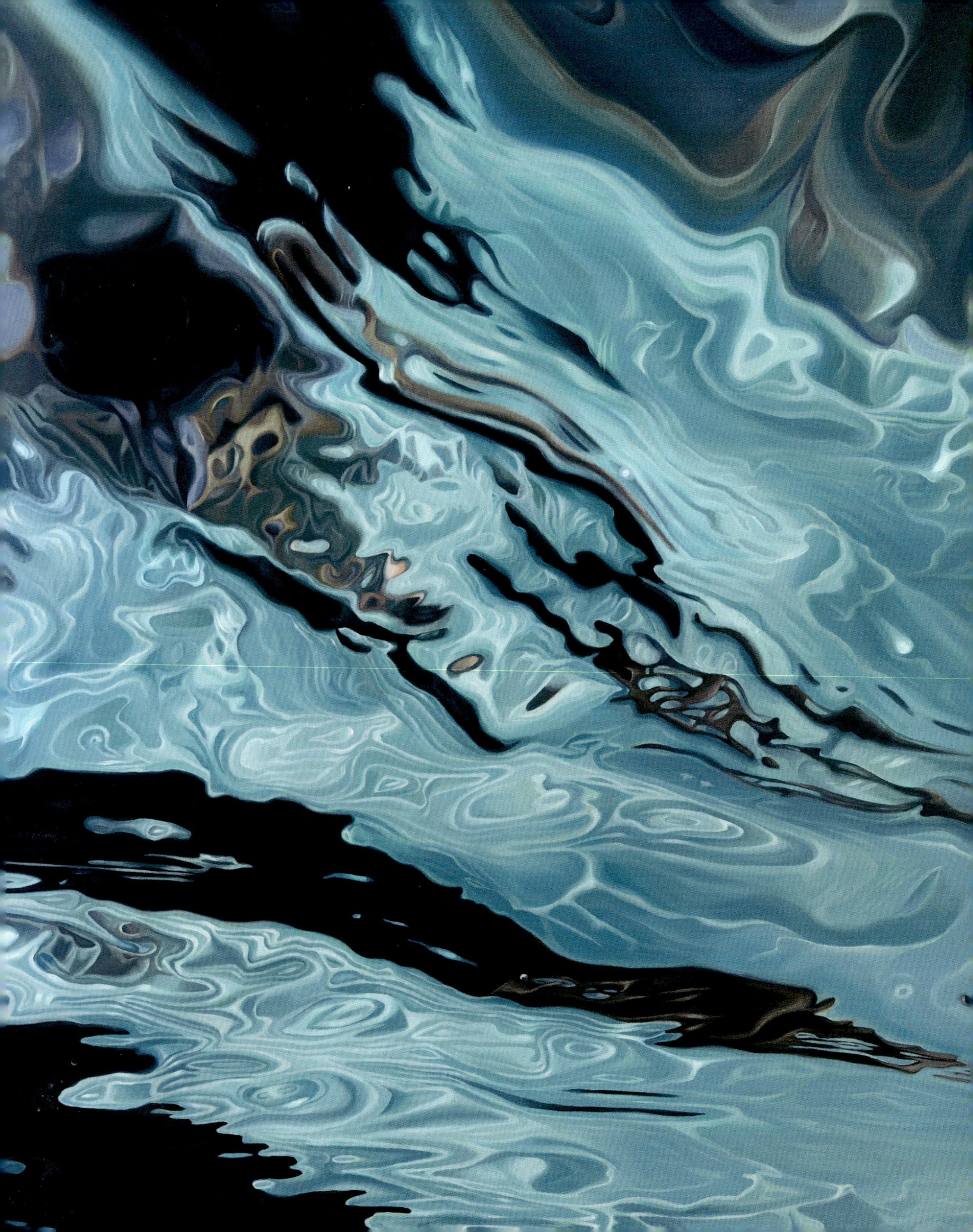

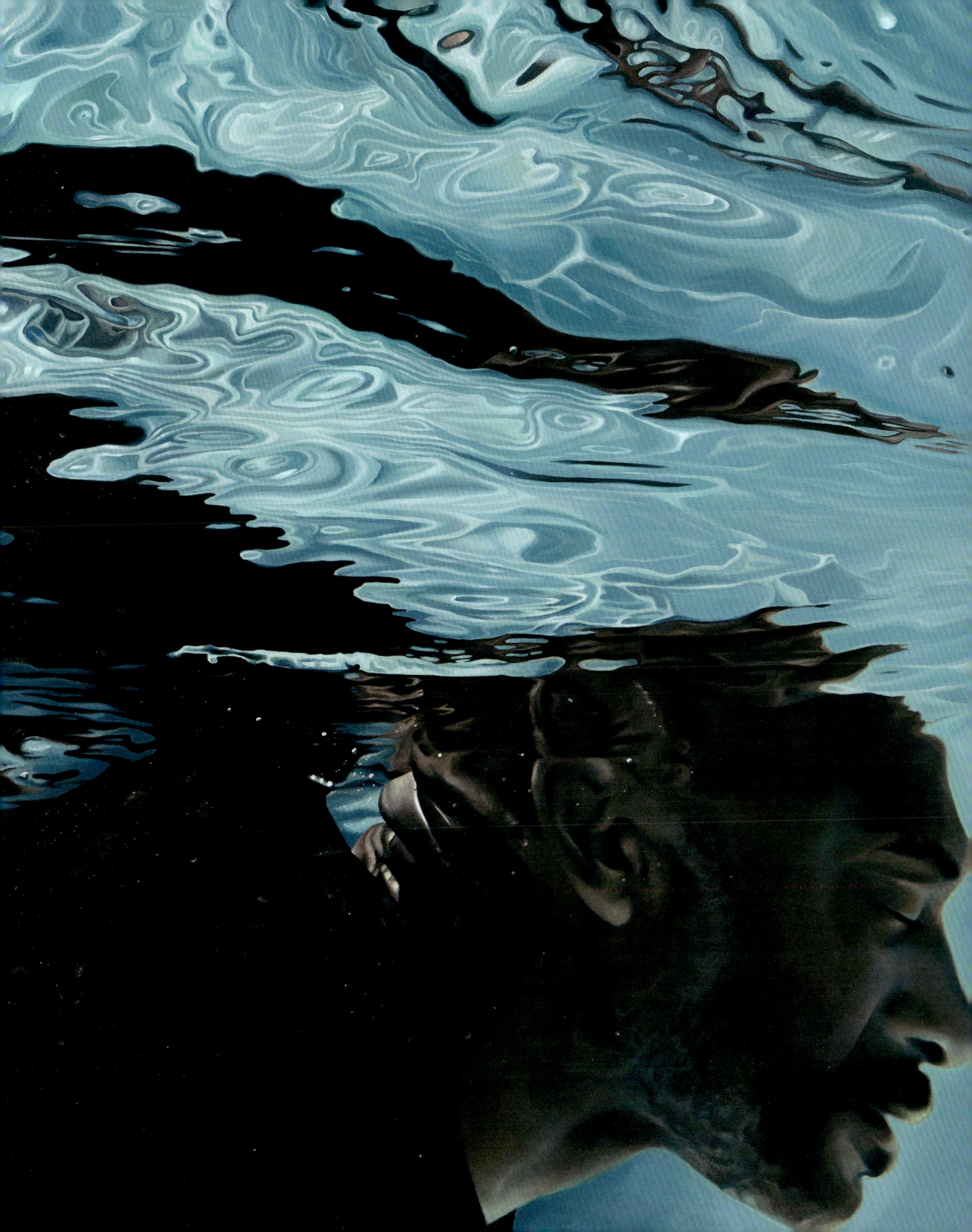

DEBORAH
ROBERTS

Combining collage with mixed media, Deborah Roberts' figurative works depict the complexity of Black subjecthood and explore themes of race, identity, and gender politics. Roberts' use of collage reflects the challenges encountered by young Black children as they strive to build their identity, particularly as they respond to preconceived social constructs perpetuated by the Black community, the white gaze, and visual culture at large. Combining a range of different facial features, skin tones, hairstyles, and clothes, Roberts explains that, through collage, she can "create a more expansive and inclusive view of the Black cultural experience."

Roberts (b. 1962, Austin, TX; lives and works in Austin, TX) launched her monograph, *20 Years of Art/Work* (published by Radius Books), during her solo exhibition, *What about us?*, at Stephen Friedman Gallery's new space in Tribeca, New York, in November 2023. Other recent solo and two-person exhibitions include those at SITE Santa Fe, NM (2023); McNay Art Museum, San Antonio, TX (2022); and The Bluecoat, Liverpool, UK (2021). The artist's major touring exhibition, *I'm*, opened at The Contemporary Austin, TX, in January 2021, following the installation of her first outdoor public mural there in September 2020. The show traveled to the Museum of Contemporary Art Denver, CO; Art + Practice in collaboration with the California African American Museum, Los Angeles, CA; and Cummer Museum of Art and Gardens, Jacksonville, FL (2021–22).

Her work featured in the touring group exhibition *Multiplicity: Blackness in Contemporary American Collage*, which opened at the Frist Art Museum, Nashville, TN (2023). Other group projects have taken place at the Institute of Contemporary Art Boston, MA (2022); Hirshhorn Museum and Sculpture Garden, Washington, DC (2022); Modern Art Museum of Fort Worth, TX (2022); Virginia Museum of Fine Arts, Richmond, VA (2021); Scottish National Galleries, Edinburgh, Scotland (2021); Van Every/Smith Galleries, Davidson College, NC (2020); Pérez Art Museum Miami, FL (2020); Massachusetts Museum of Contemporary Art, North Adams, MA (2019); Somerset House, London, UK (2019); and the Studio Museum in Harlem, NY (2017).

Roberts' work is held in significant public collections including Scottish National Galleries, Edinburgh, UK; Dallas Museum of Art, TX; Hammer Museum, Los Angeles, CA; Hirshhorn Museum and Sculpture Garden, Washington, DC; Museum of Fine Arts, Boston, MA; Solomon R. Guggenheim Museum, New York, NY; and the Whitney Museum of American Art, New York, NY.

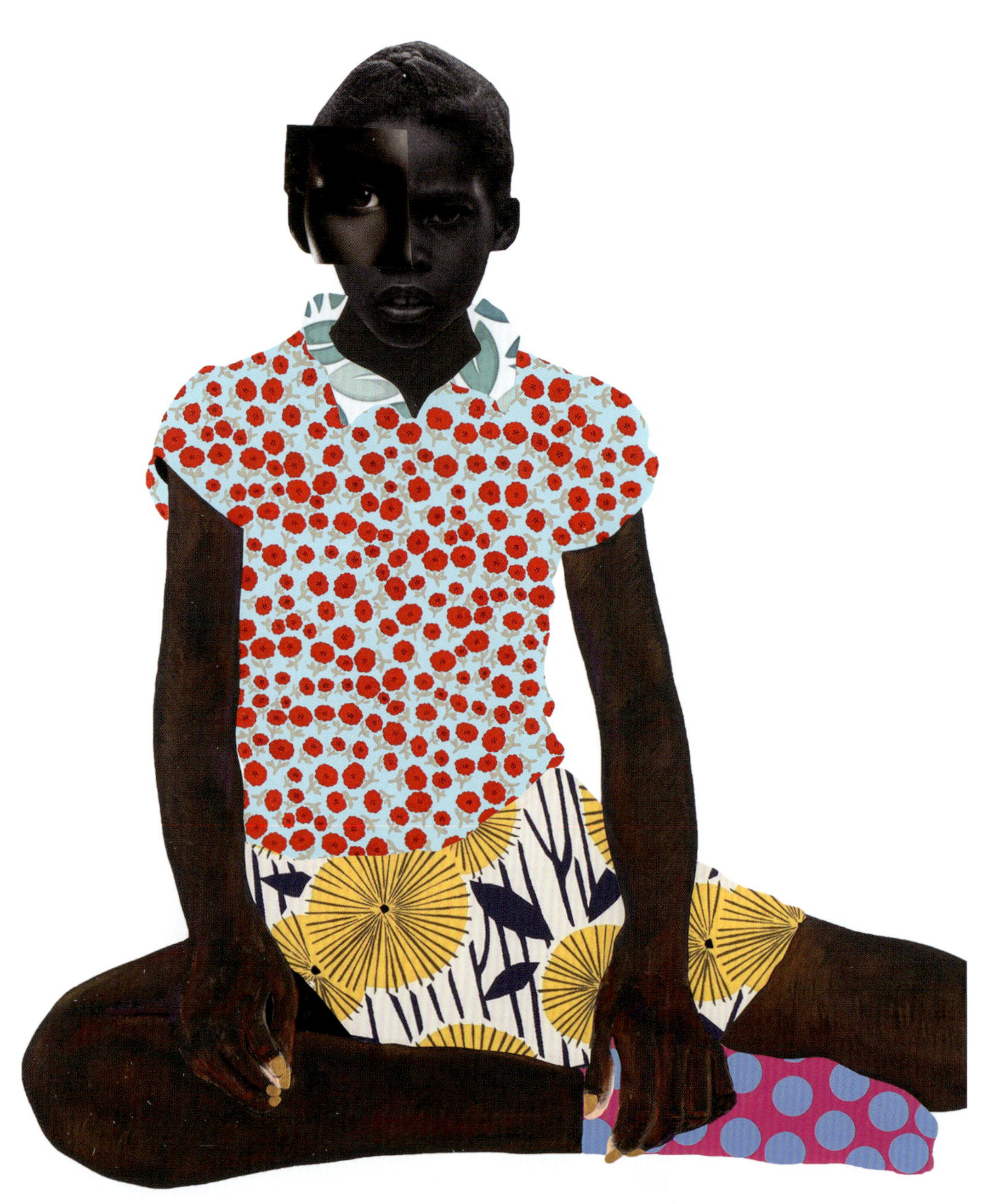

Delilah, 2021
Mixed media and collage on canvas
65 × 45 inches

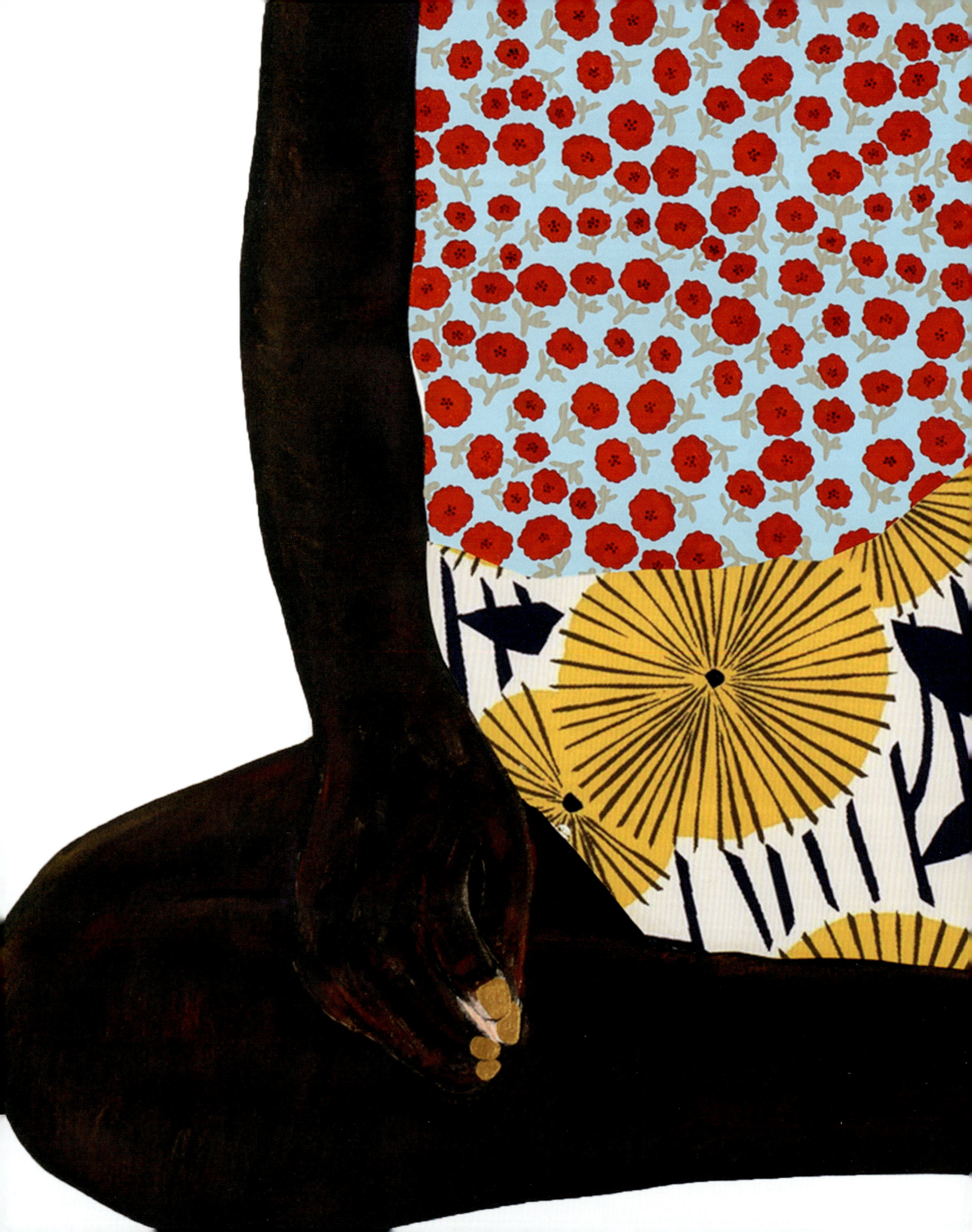

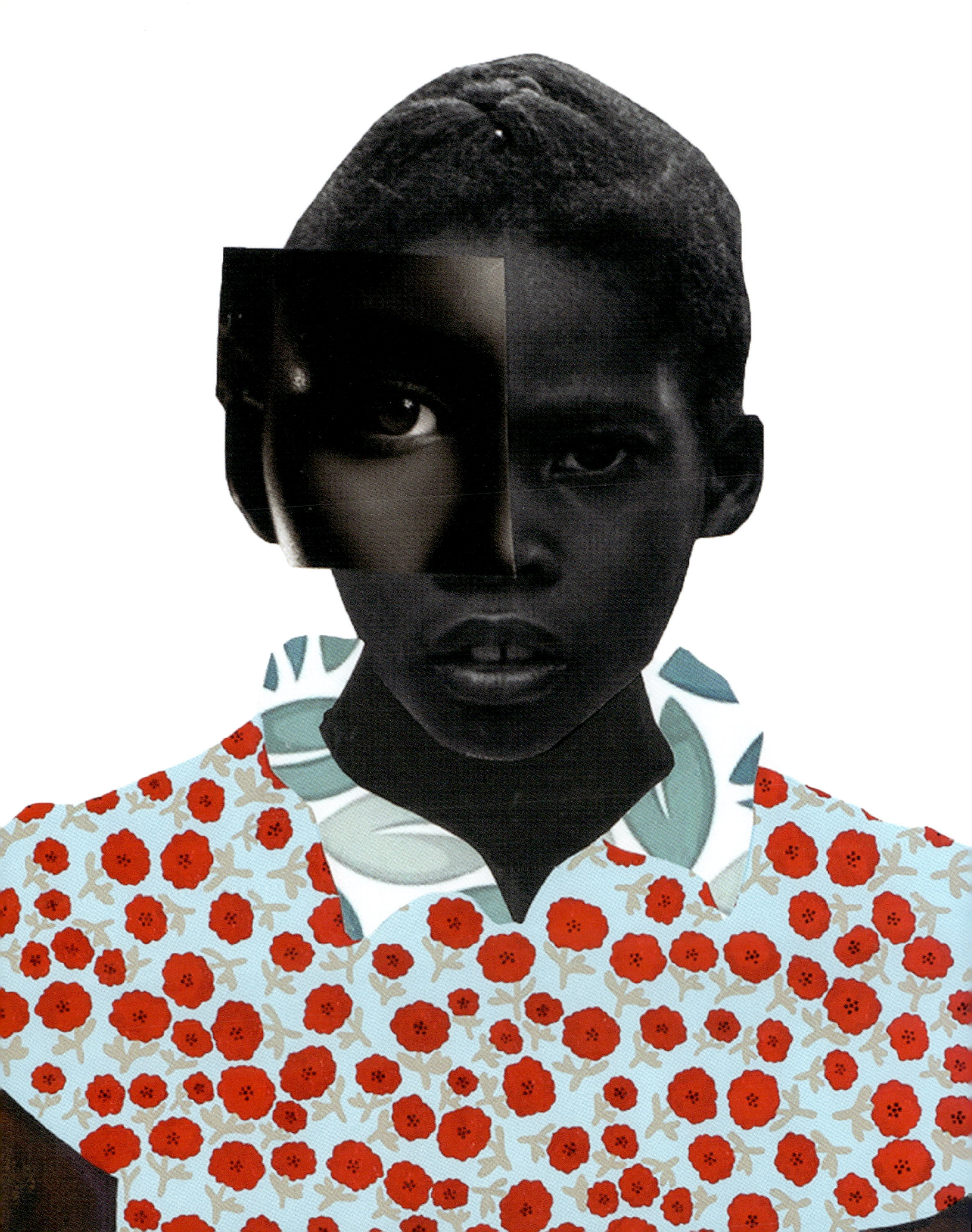

Let me tell you this again and again, 2020
Mixed media and collage on paper
52 × 38 inches

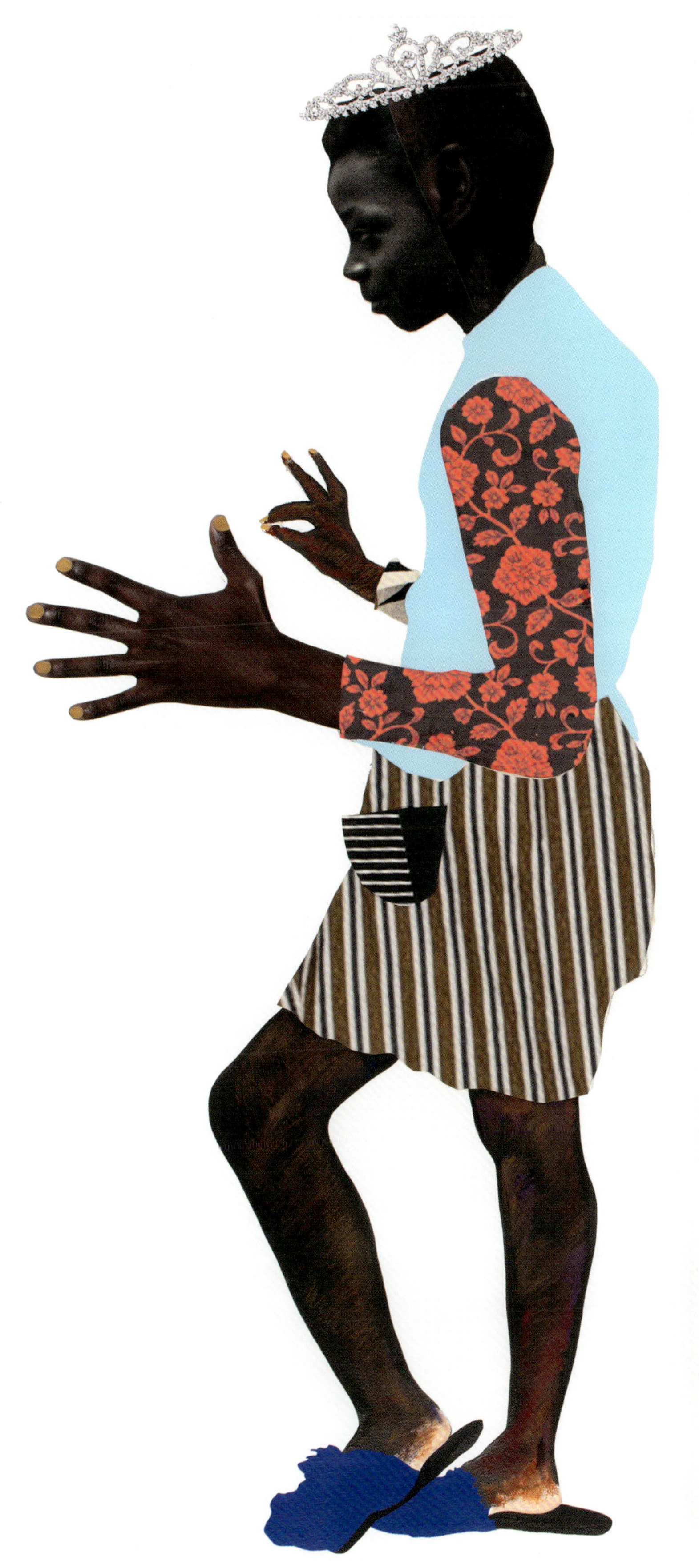

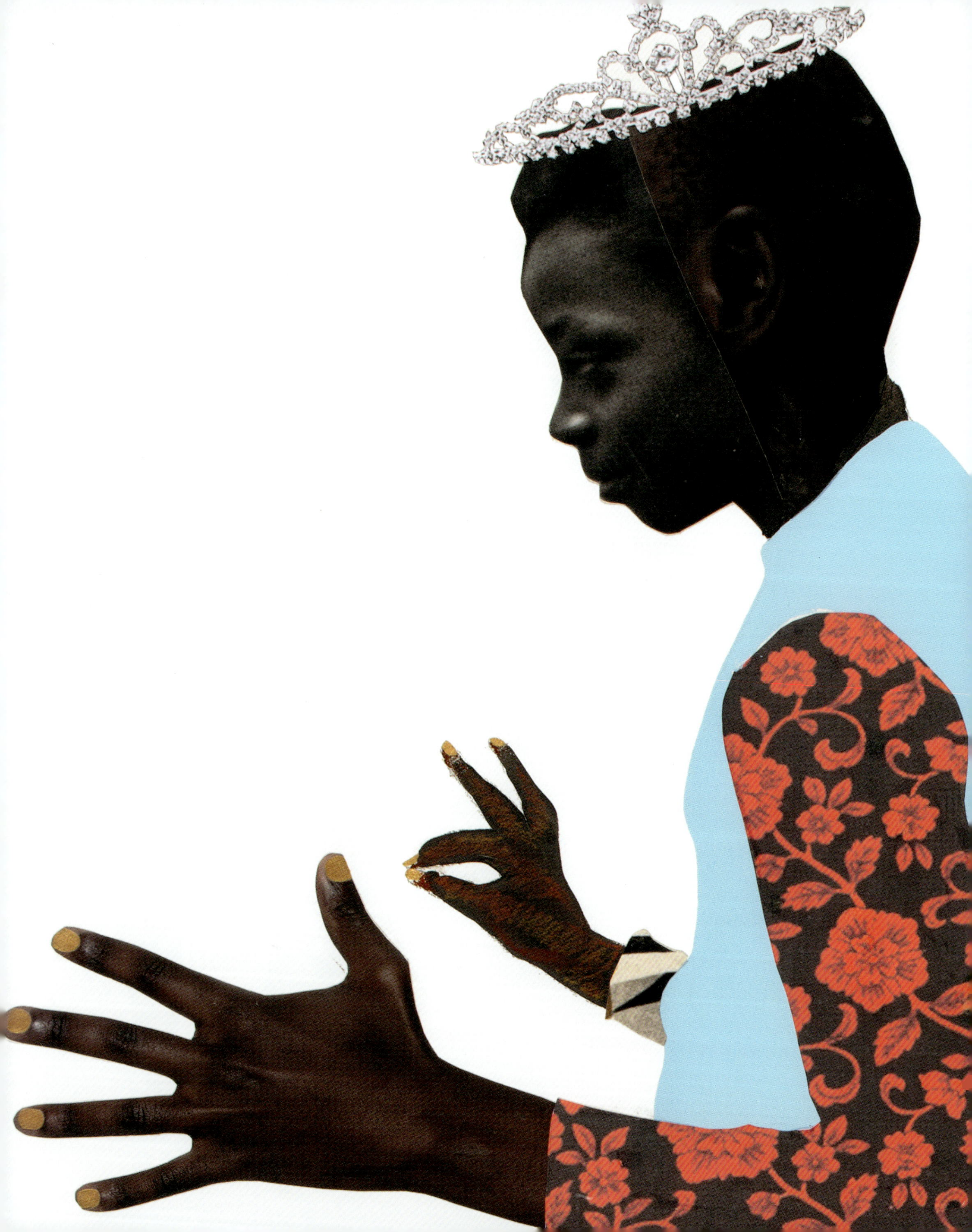

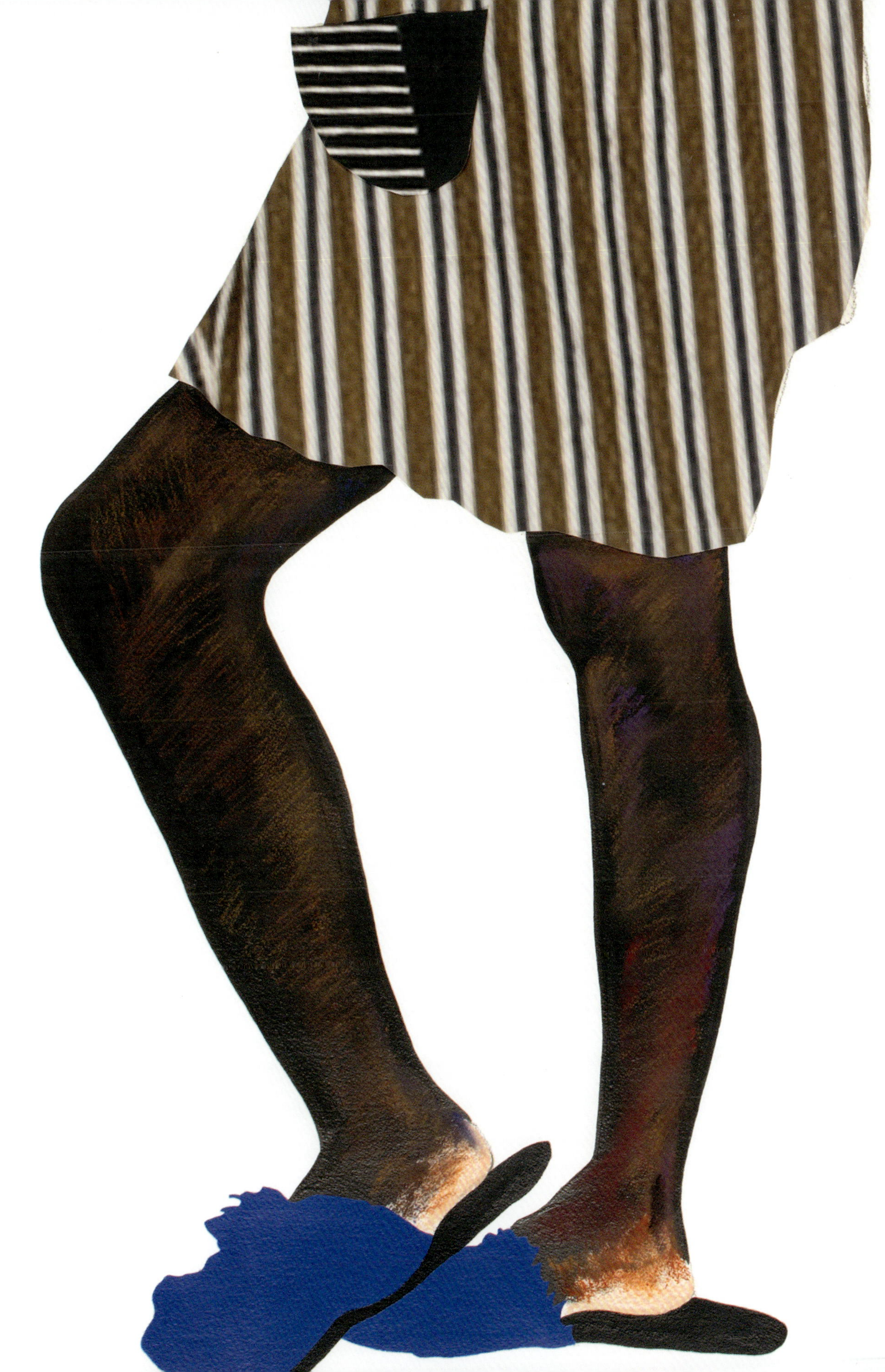

TSCHABALALA
SELF

Tschabalala Self builds a singular style from the syncretic use of both painting and printmaking to explore ideas about the Black body. She constructs depictions of predominantly female bodies using a combination of sewn, printed, and painted materials, traversing different artistic and craft traditions. The formal and conceptual aspects of Self's work seek to expand her critical inquiry into selfhood and human flourishing.

Self (b. 1990, Harlem, NY; lives and works in the Hudson Valley, NY) has had her work featured in numerous exhibitions at institutions including FLAG Art Foundation, New York, NY (2024); Barbican, London, UK (2024); Brooklyn Museum, NY (2024); CC Strombeek, Grimbergen, Belgium (2023); Desert X, Coachella Valley, CA (2023); Kunstmuseum St. Gallen, Switzerland (2023); Le Consortium, Dijon, France (2022); Performa 2021, New York, NY (2021); Haus der Kunst, Munich, Germany (2021); Kunsthalle Düsseldorf, Germany (2021); and Baltimore Museum of Art, MD (2021); amongst many others.

Red Room, 2022
Crushed velvet, fabric, acrylic, flashe, spray paint,
thread, and painted canvas on canvas
94 × 84 × 1½ inches

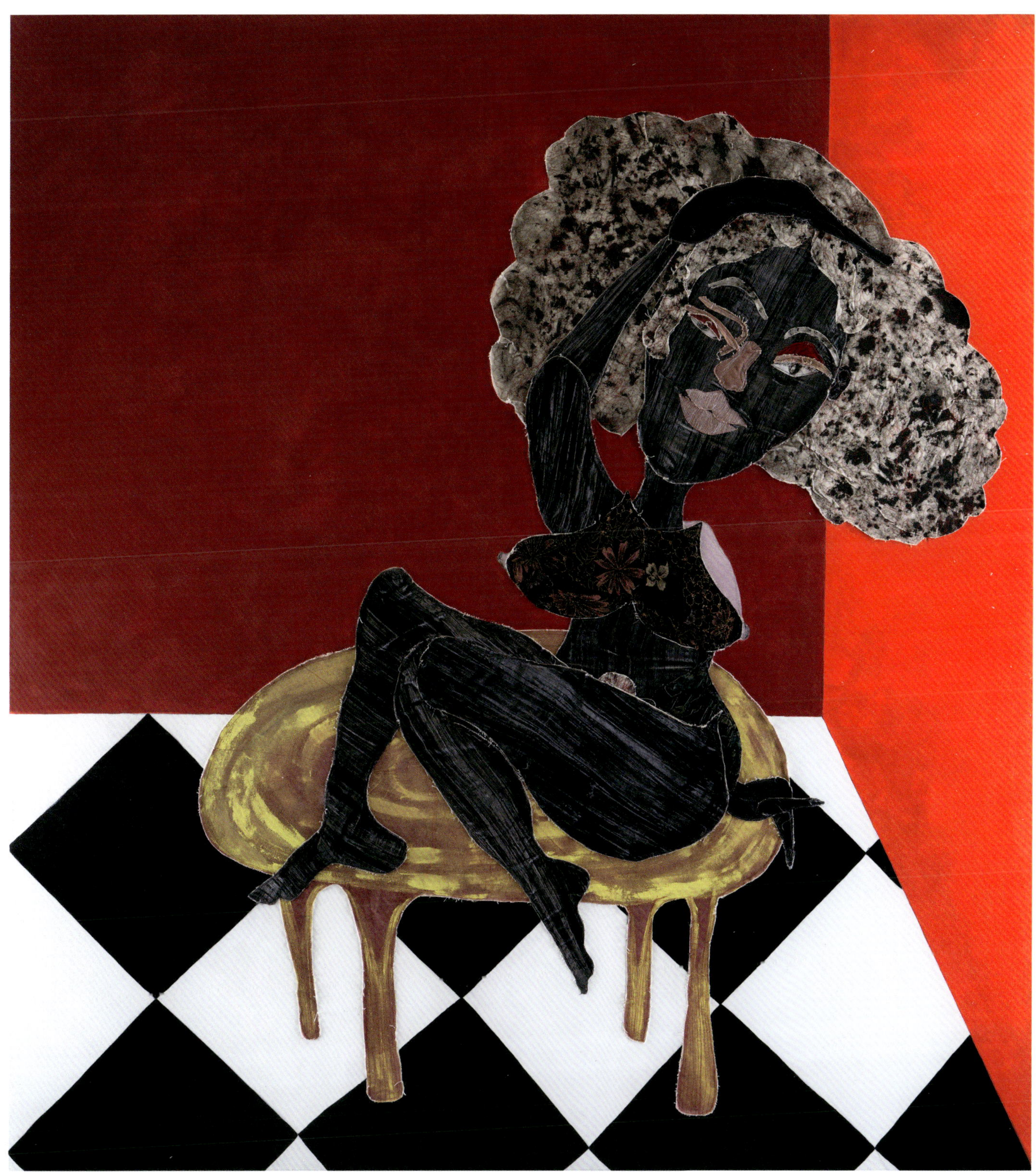

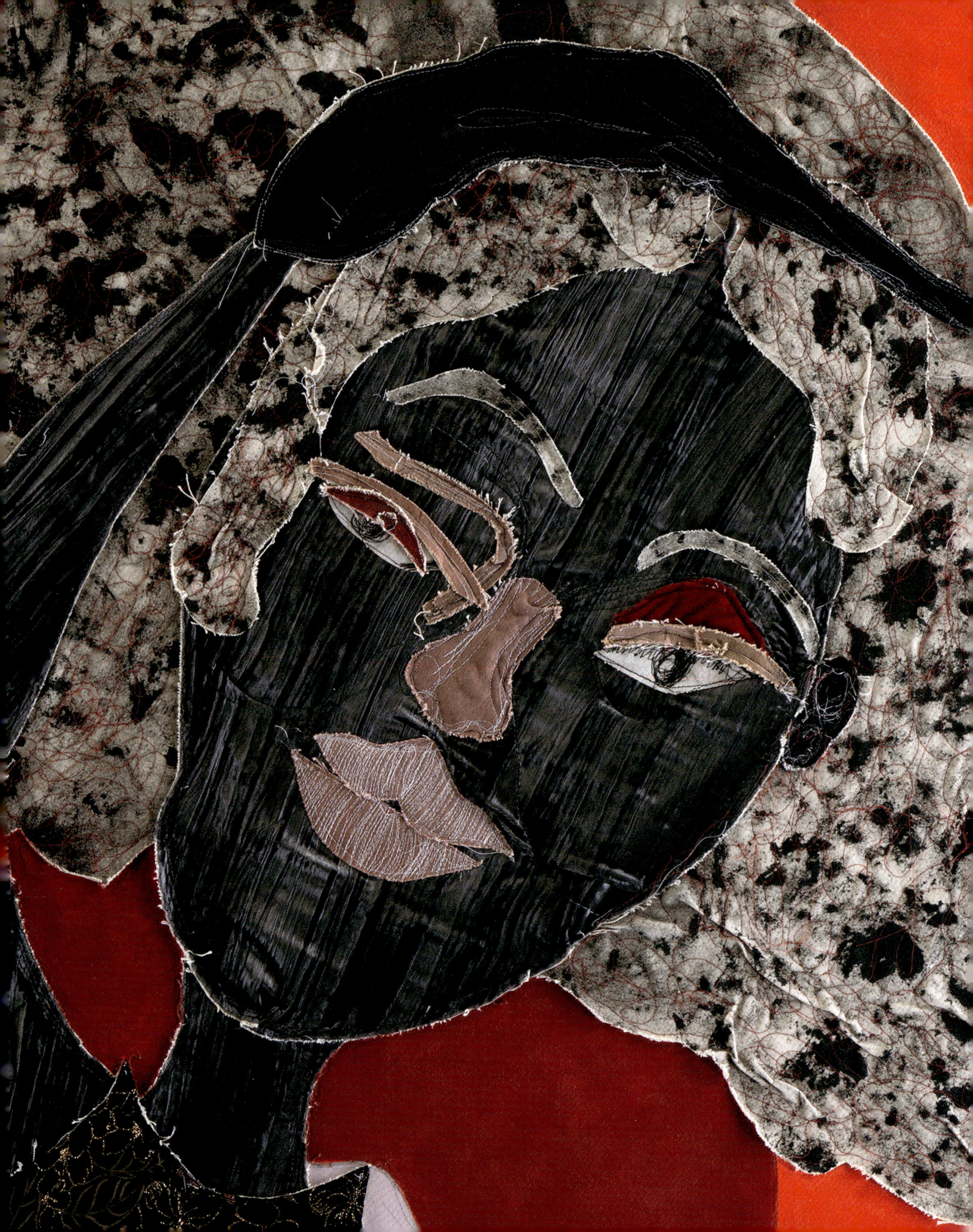

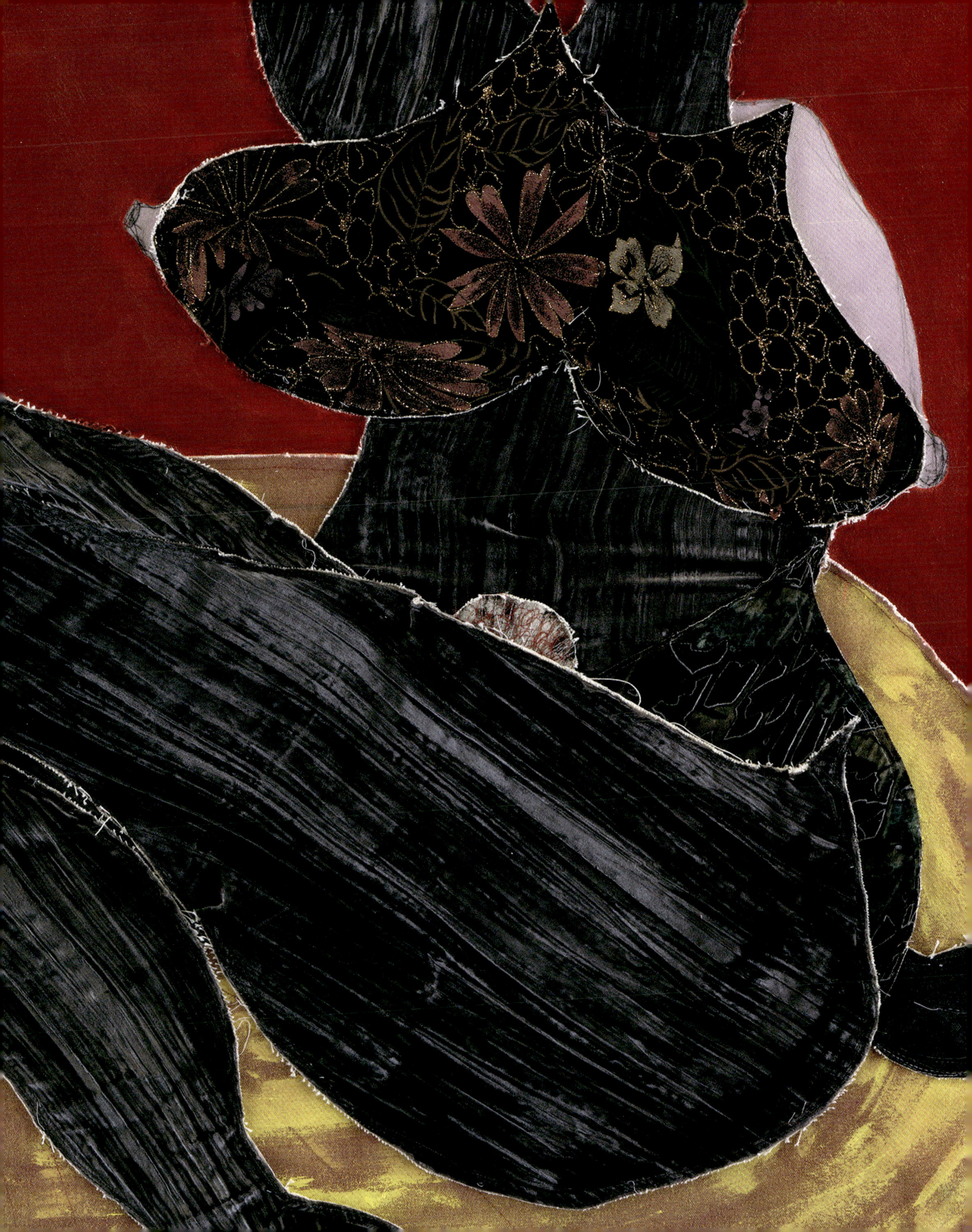

AMY
SHERALD

Amy Sherald documents the contemporary African American experience in the United States through arresting, intimate portraits. Sherald engages with the history of photography and portraiture, inviting viewers to participate in a more complex debate about accepted notions of race and representation and to situate Black life in American art.

Sherald (b. 1973, Columbus, GA; lives and works in the New York City area) received her MFA in painting from Maryland Institute College of Art and her BA in painting from Clark Atlanta University. Sherald was the first woman and first African American to ever receive the grand prize in the Outwin Boochever Portrait Competition from the National Portrait Gallery in Washington, DC; she also received the 2017 Anonymous Was A Woman Award and the 2018 Smithsonian Ingenuity Award. In 2018, Sherald was selected by First Lady Michelle Obama to paint her portrait as an official commission for the National Portrait Gallery in Washington, DC. The same year, she was also awarded the Pollock Prize for Creativity by the Pollock-Krasner Foundation, as well as the David C. Driskell Prize from the High Museum of Art, Atlanta, GA.

Sherald's work is held in public collections such as the Crystal Bridges Museum of American Art, Bentonville, AR; Embassy of the United States, Dakar, Senegal; Los Angeles County Museum of Art, CA; Museum of Fine Arts, Boston, MA; Nasher Museum of Art, Durham, NC; San Francisco Museum of Modern Art, CA; Smithsonian National Museum of African American History and Culture, Washington, DC; Smithsonian National Portrait Gallery, Washington, DC; and the Whitney Museum of American Art, New York, NY.

The Rabbit in the Hat, 2009
Oil on canvas
54 × 43 × 2¾ inches

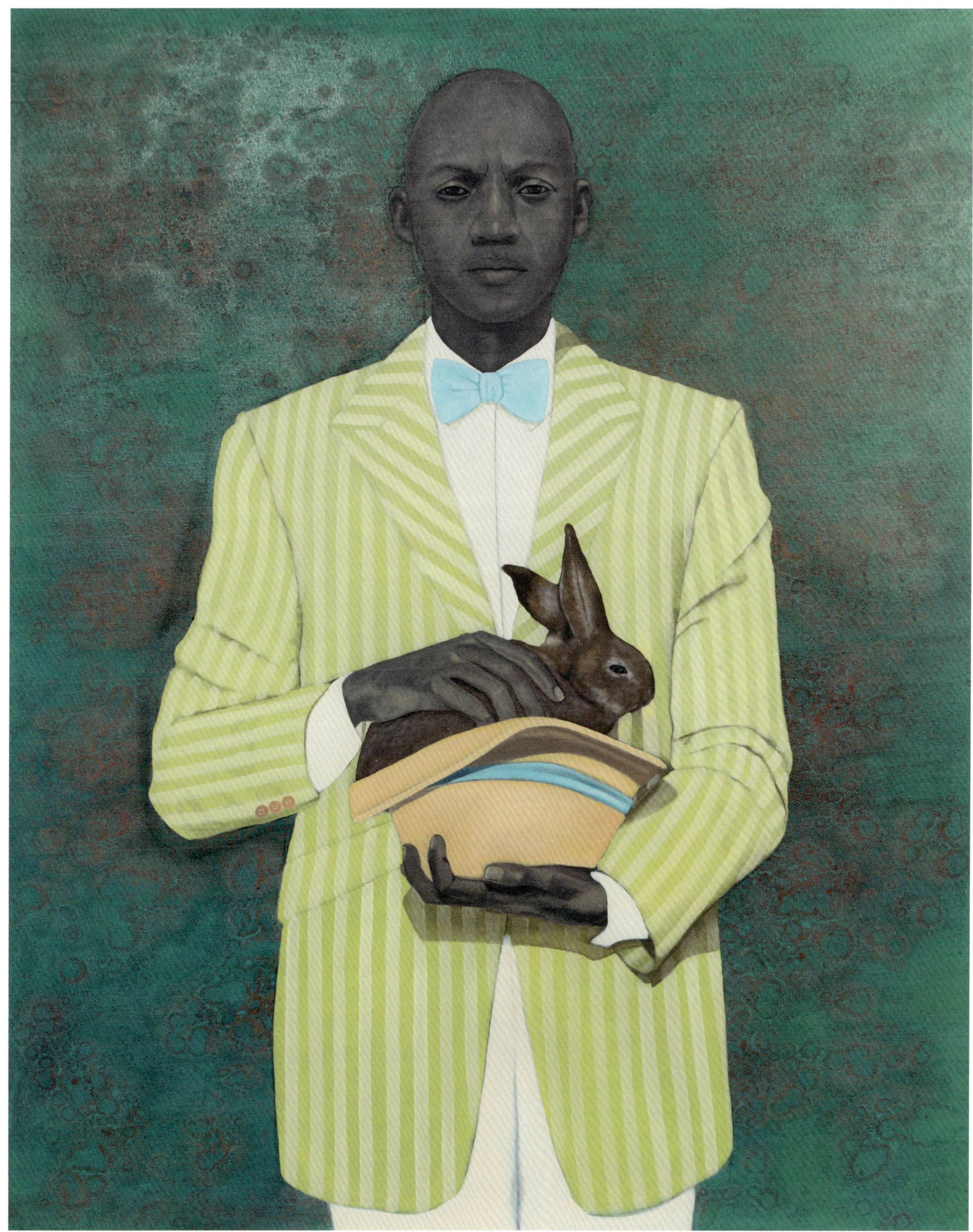

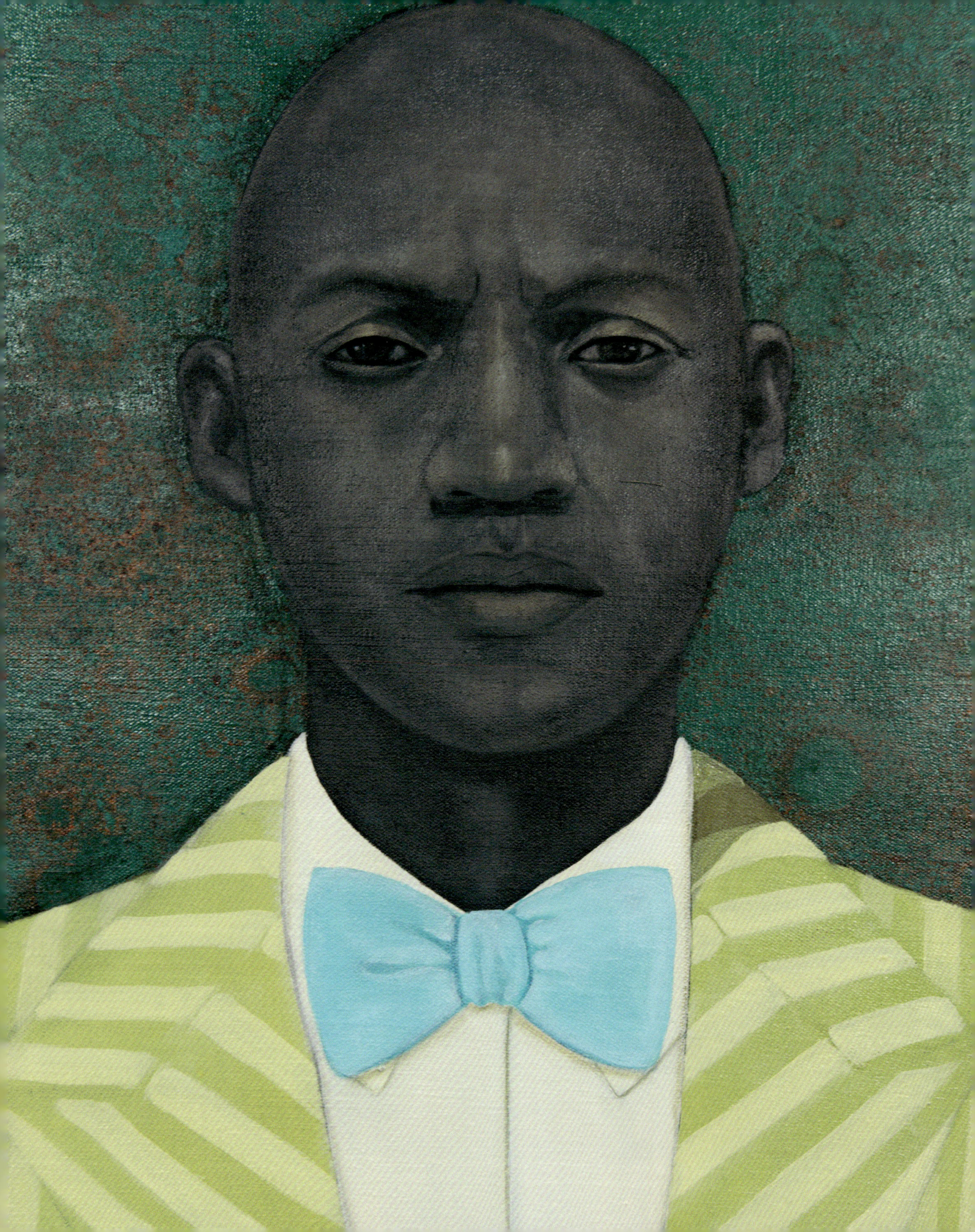

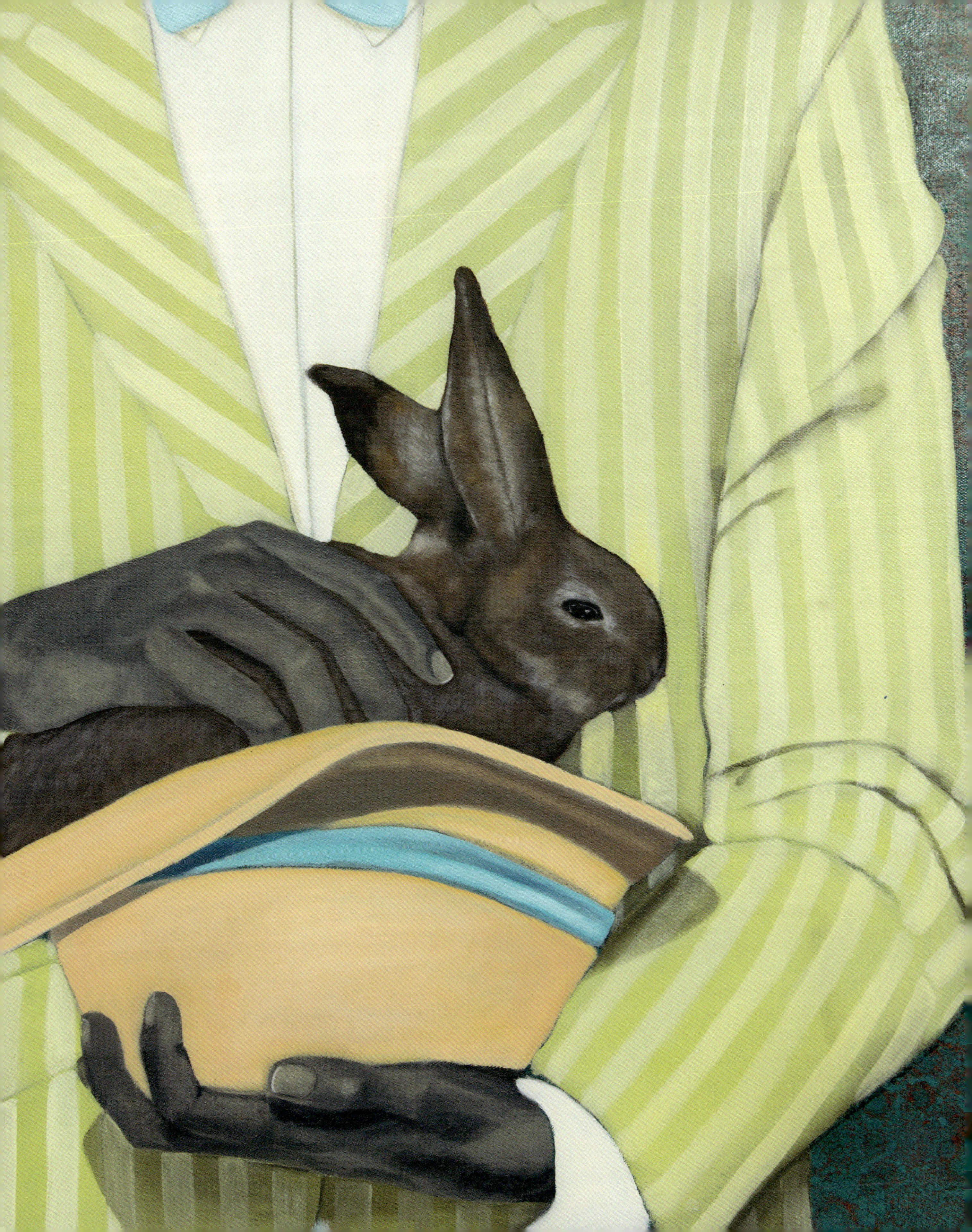

MICKALENE
THOMAS

Mickalene Thomas is an award-winning, multidisciplinary artist whose work has yielded instantly recognizable and widely celebrated aesthetic languages within contemporary visual culture. She is known for her elaborate portraits of Black women composed of rhinestones, acrylic, and enamel. Not only do her masterful mixed-media paintings, photographs, films, and installations command space, they also occupy eloquently while dissecting the intersecting complexities of Black and female identity within the Western canon.

Outside of her core practice, Thomas is a Tony Award–nominated coproducer, curator, educator, and mentor to many emerging artists. Apart from her own monumental solo shows, she simultaneously curates exhibitions at galleries and museums and collaborates with corporations and luxury brands. In 2023, she became the first Black femme artist to have a scholarship in her name at the Yale School of Art. She has also been the recipient of numerous prizes, grants, and honors, including the Creative Capital Wild Futures: Art, Culture, Impact Award (2024); Hirshhorn Artist x Artist New York Gala honoree (2023); the Pratt Institute Legends Award (2022); Rema Hort Mann Foundation 25th Anniversary honoree (2022); Artistic Impact Award, Newark Museum (2022); Glass House 15th Anniversary Artist of the Year (2022); Yale School of Art Presidential Visiting Fellow in Fine Arts (2020); Legend in Residence Award, Bronx Museum (2020); Pauli Murray College Associate Fellow at Yale University (2020); Appraisers Association of America, Award for Excellence in the Arts, (2019); Meyerhoff-Becker Biennial Commission at Baltimore Museum of Art (2019). In 2018, she received an Honorary Doctorate in Fine Arts from the New York Academy of Art and, in 2015, she was a United States Artists Francie Bishop Good & David Horvitz Fellow. Thomas is also the Cofounder of SOULAS House, a cultural hub and retreat for Black women, the Cofounder of Pratt>FORWARD, and founder of Art>FORWARD Artist in the Market incubator for postgraduate students.

Work by Thomas is in the collections of numerous institutions, including the Museum of Modern Art, New York; Whitney Museum of American Art, New York; Brooklyn Museum, NY; Studio Museum in Harlem, NY; International Center of Photography, New York; National Gallery of Art, Washington, DC; National Portrait Gallery, Smithsonian Institution, Washington, DC; National Museum of Women in the Arts, Washington, DC; Art Institute of Chicago; San Francisco Museum of Modern Art; Montreal Museum of Fine Arts; the Metropolitan Museum of Art, New York; and the J. Paul Getty Museum, Los Angeles; among others. Thomas serves on the Board of Trustees for the Brooklyn Museum and MoMA PS1.

Clarivel Face Forward Gazing, 2024
Rhinestones, acrylic, and oil paint on
canvas mounted on wood panel
96 × 144 inches

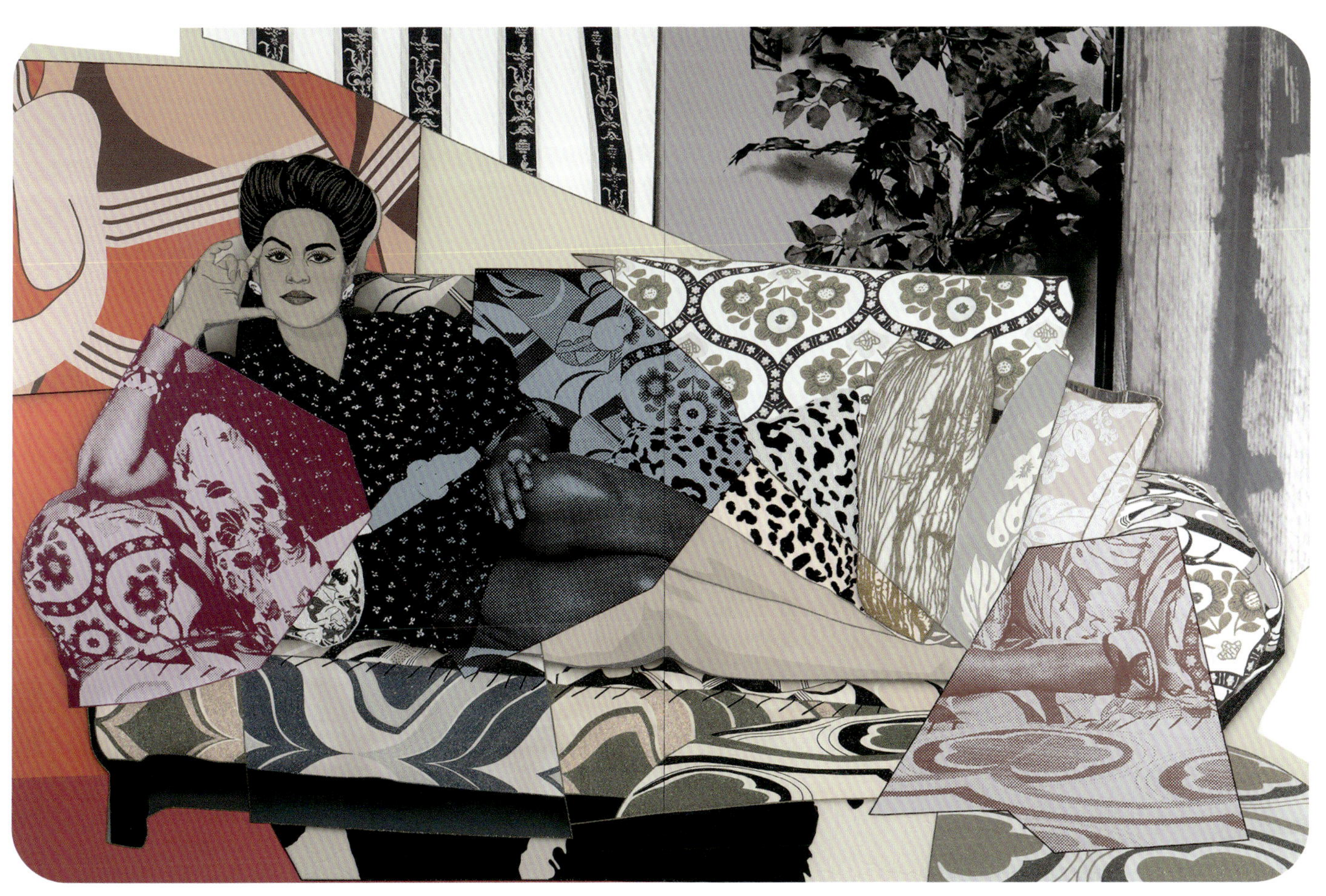

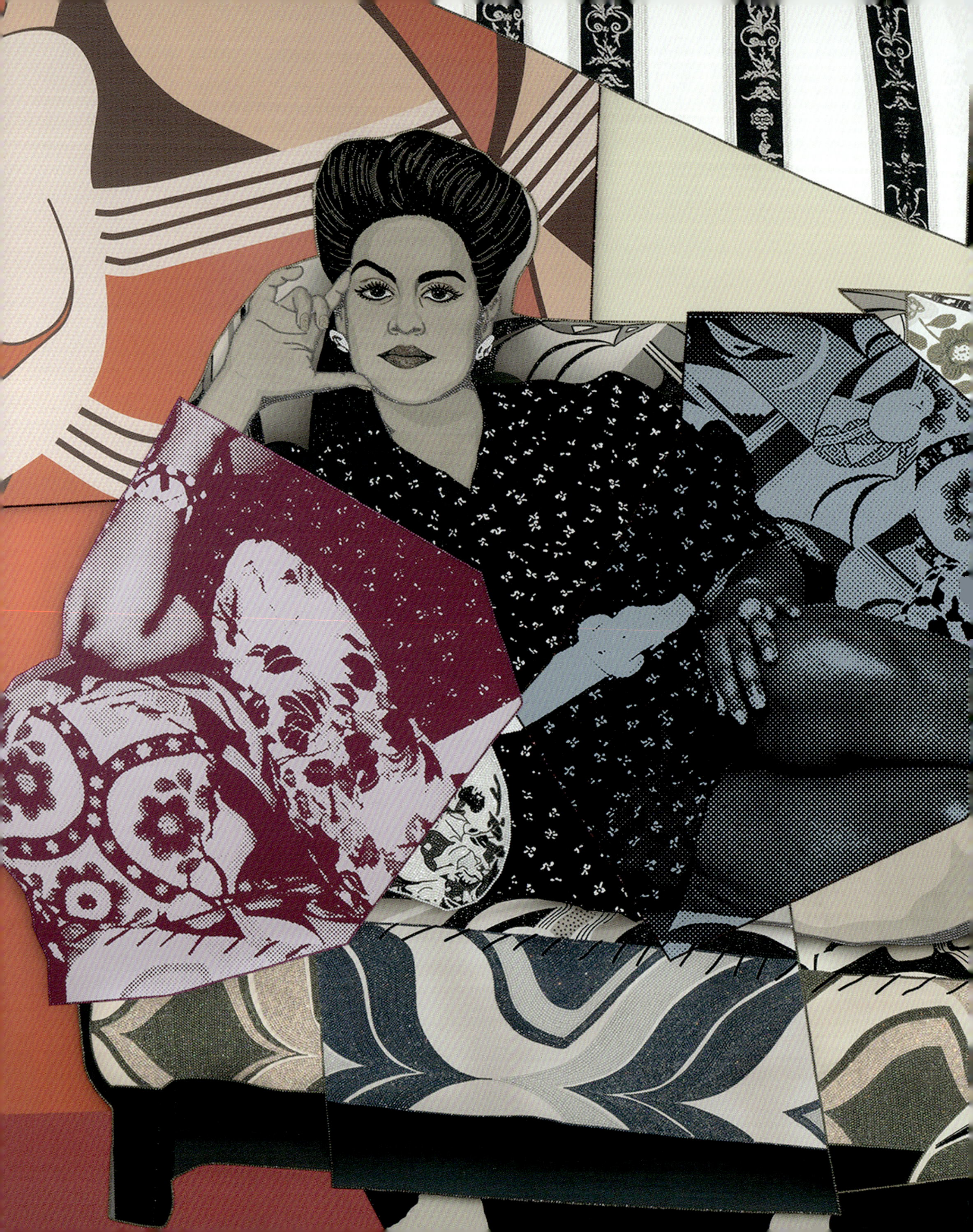

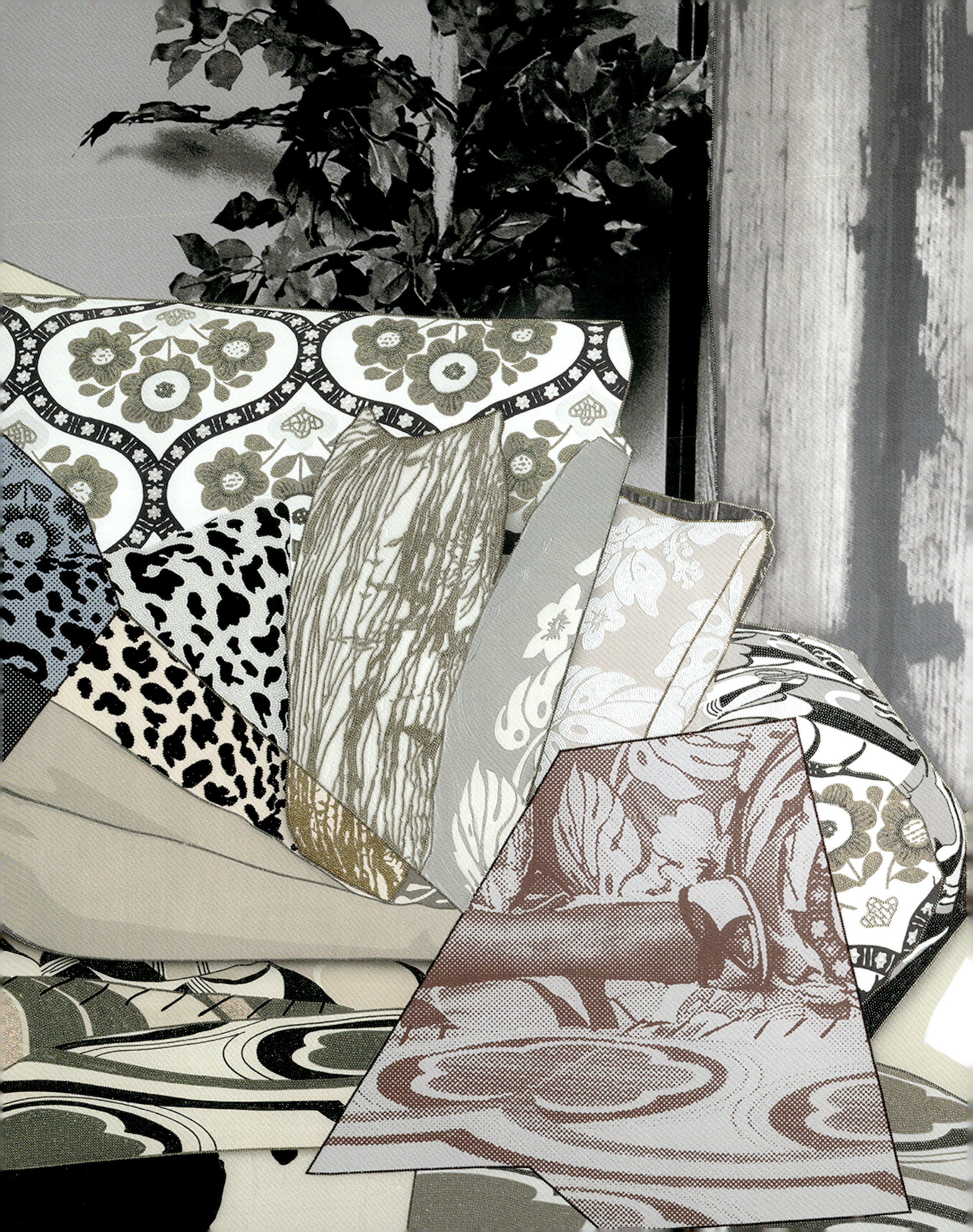

LYNETTE
YIADOM-BOAKYE

6pm Madeira, 2011
Oil on canvas
70⅞ × 59 inches

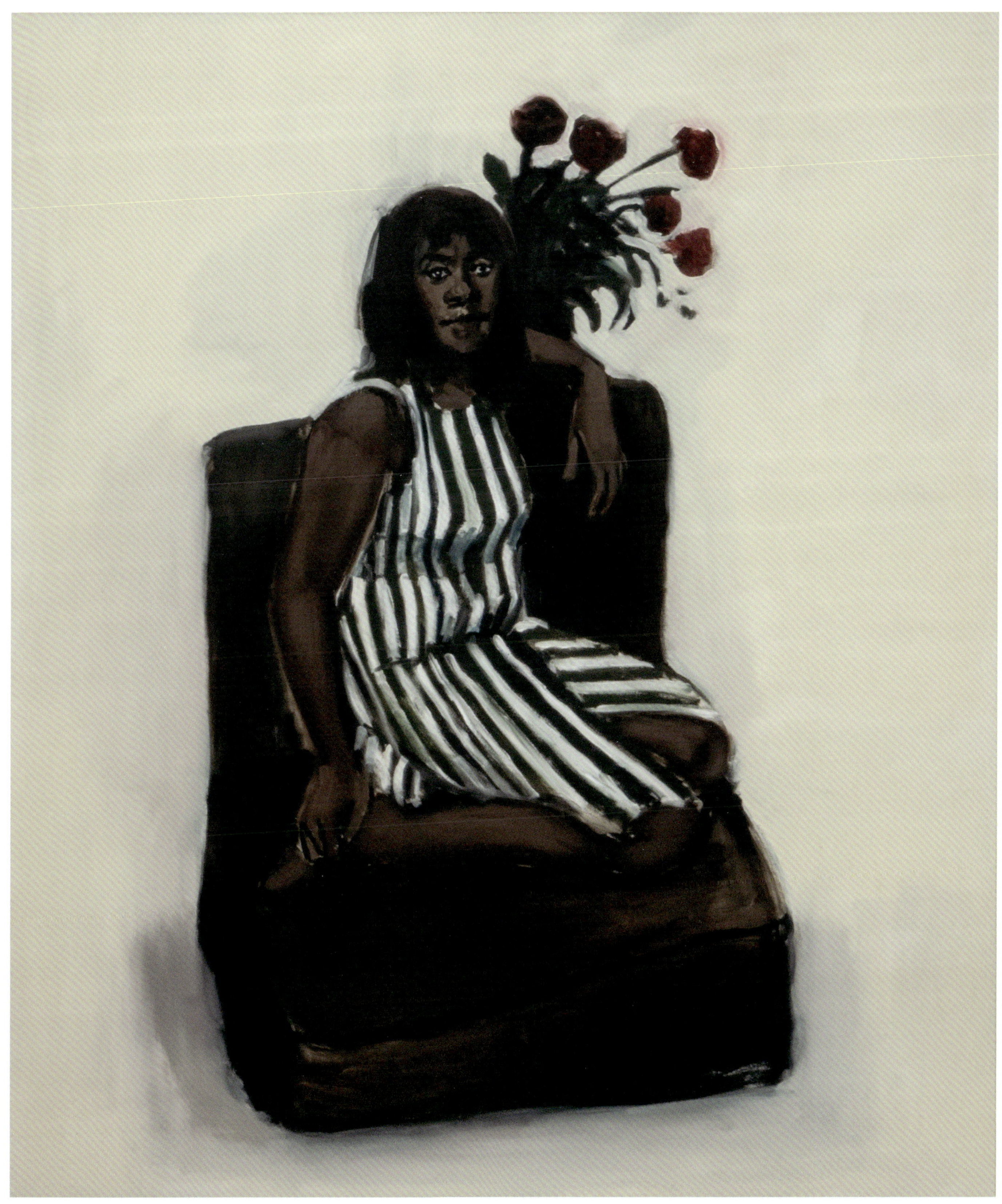

EXHIBITION
IMAGES

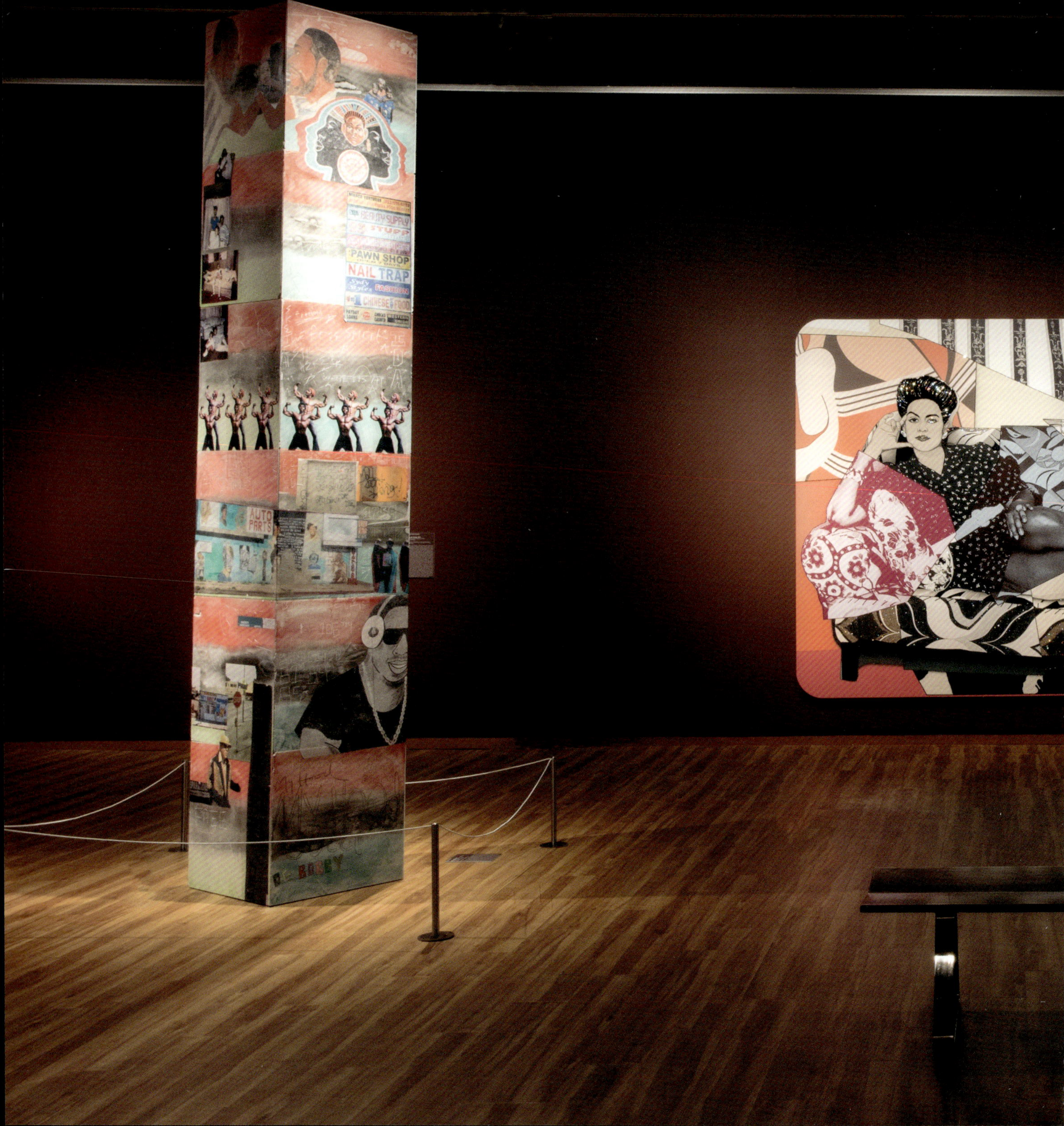
BEAUTY SUPPLY
STUFF
PAWN SHOP
NAIL TRAP
FASHION
CHINESE FOOD
AUTO PARTS

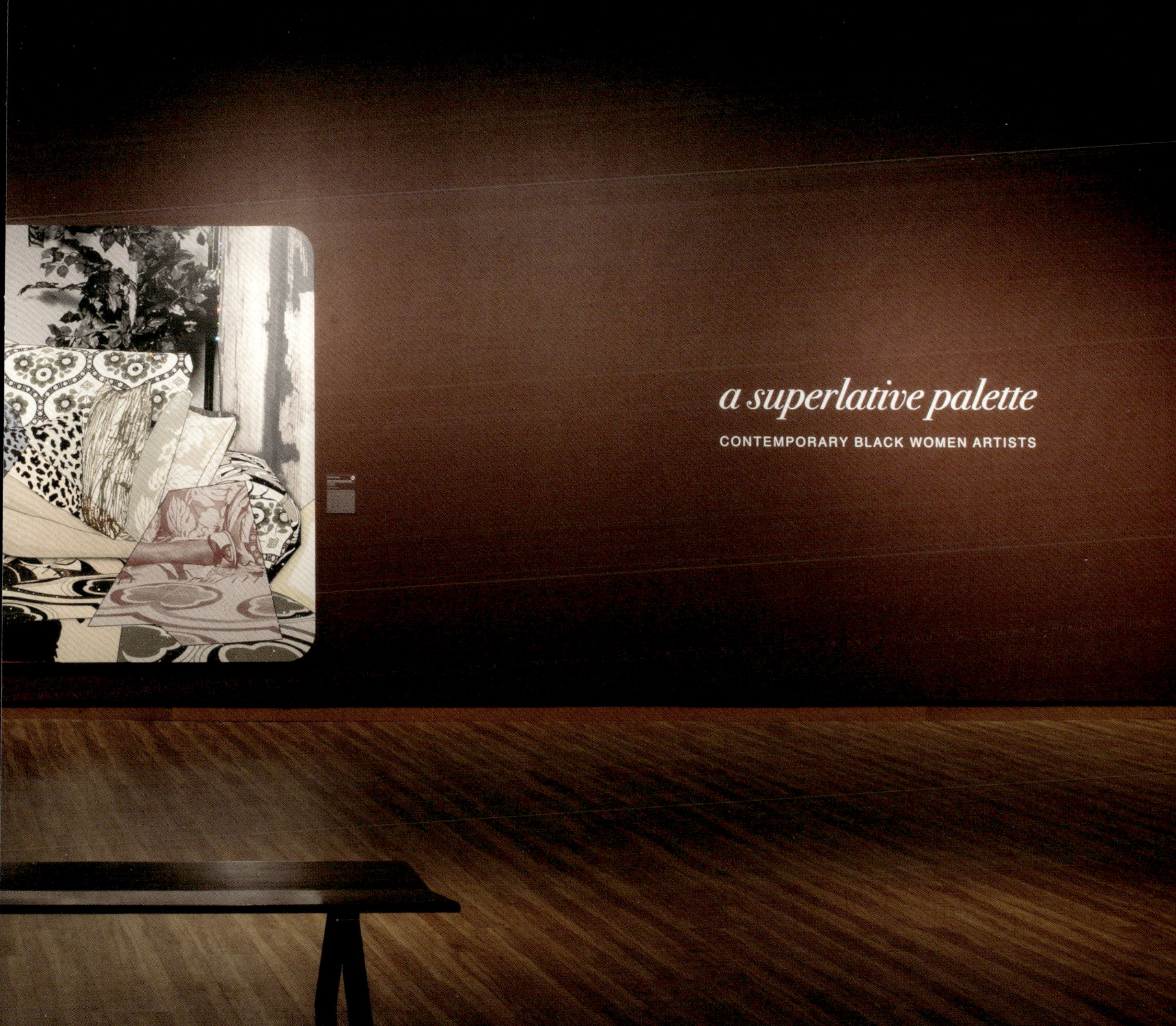

a superlative palette
CONTEMPORARY BLACK WOMEN ARTISTS

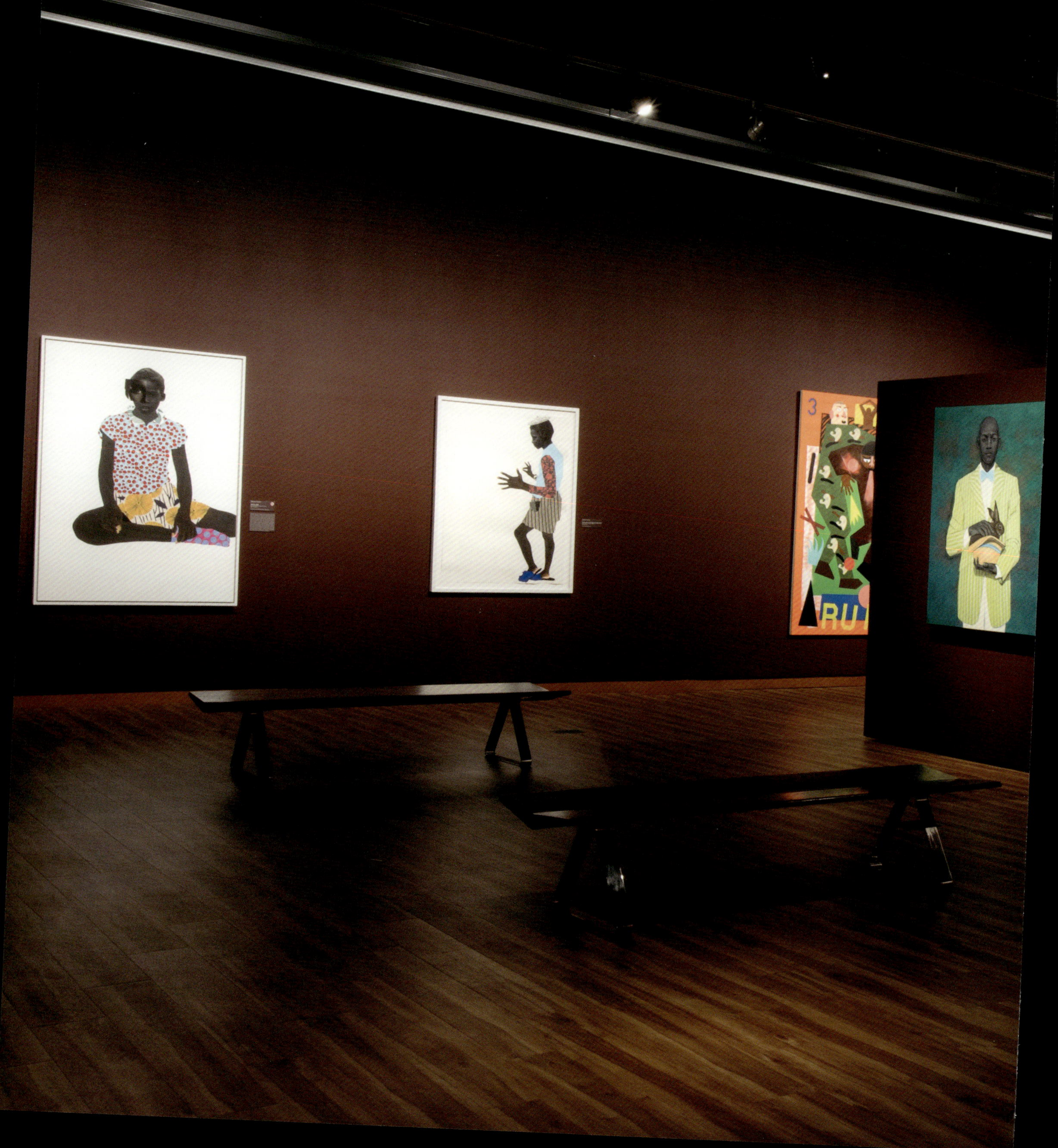

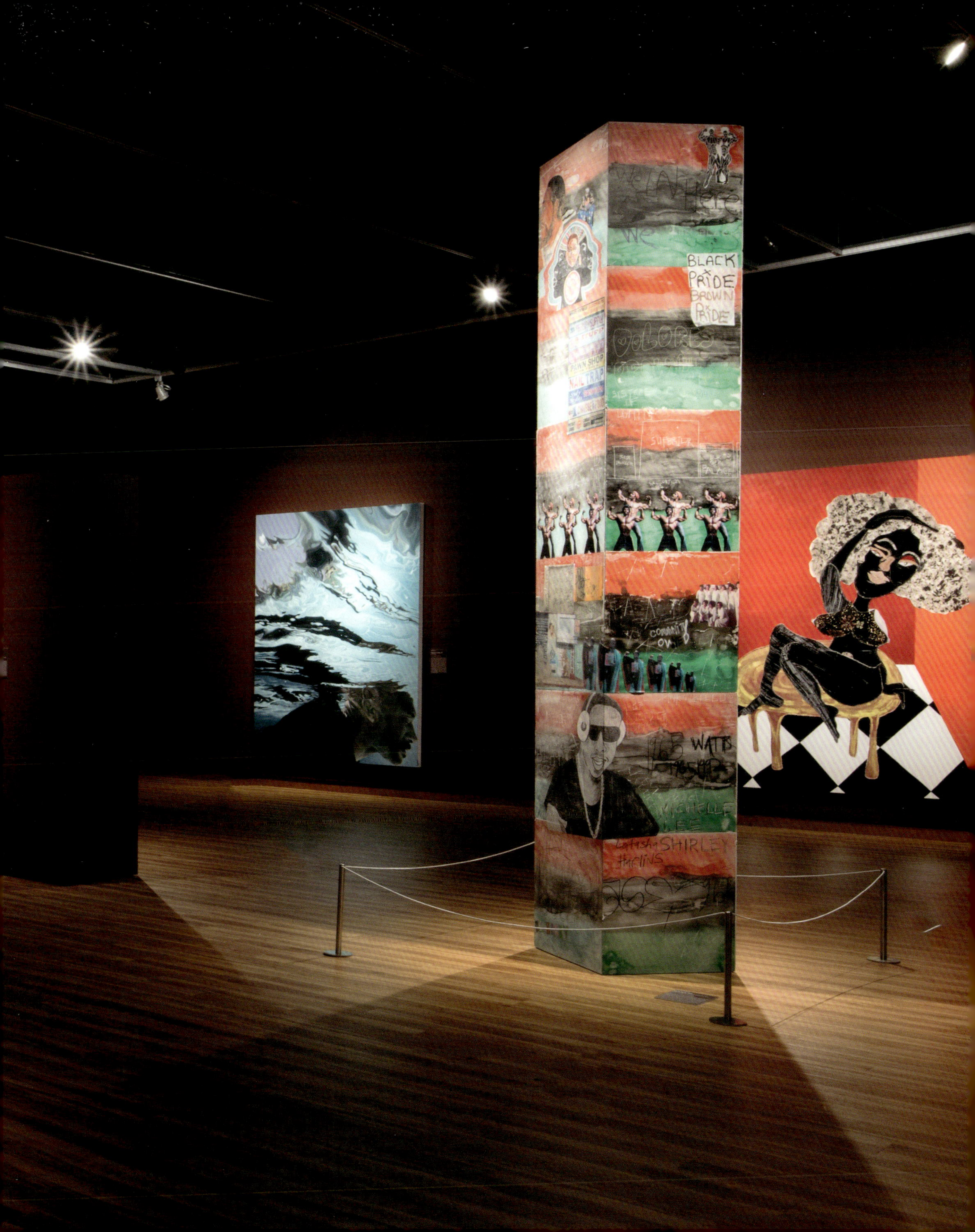

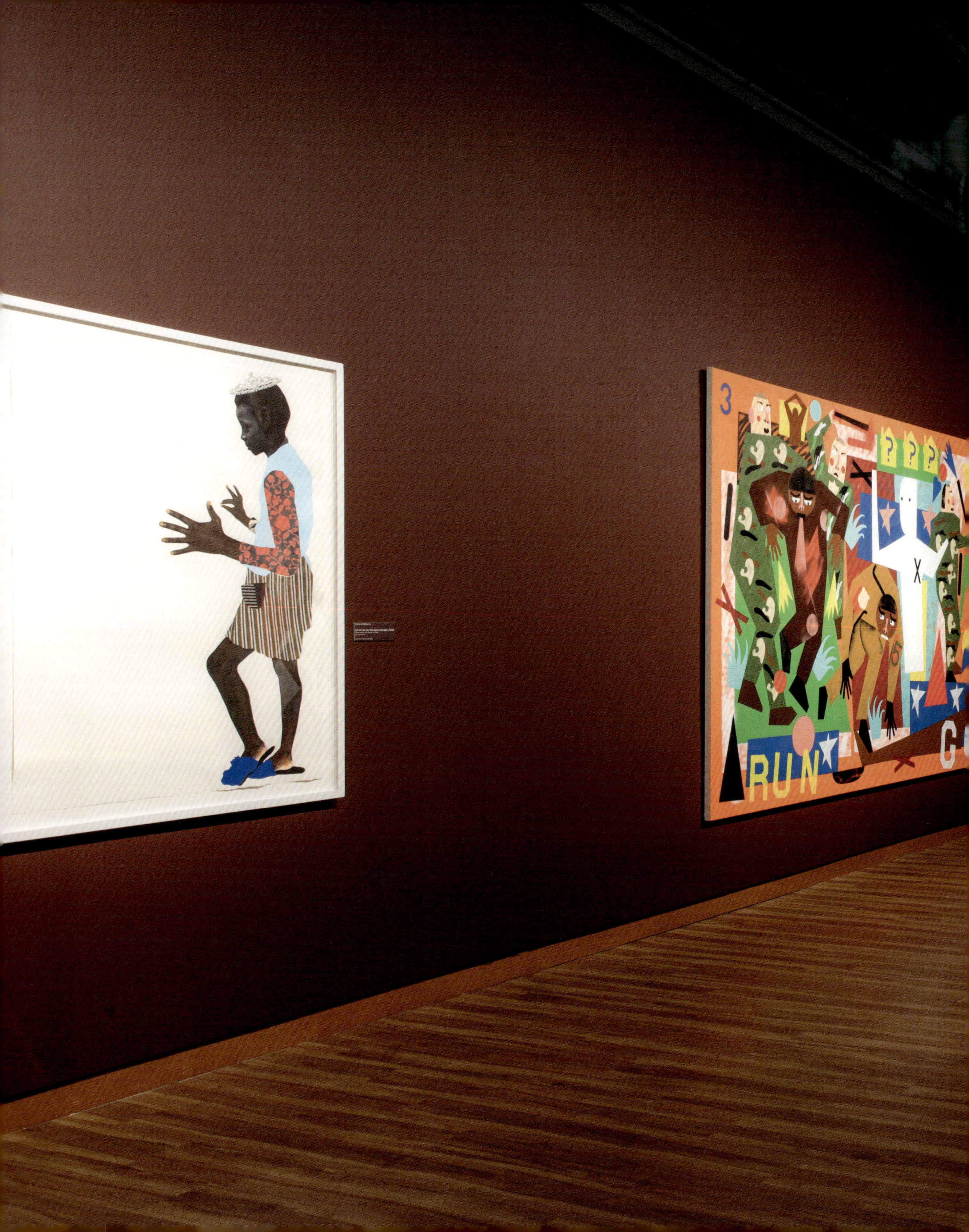

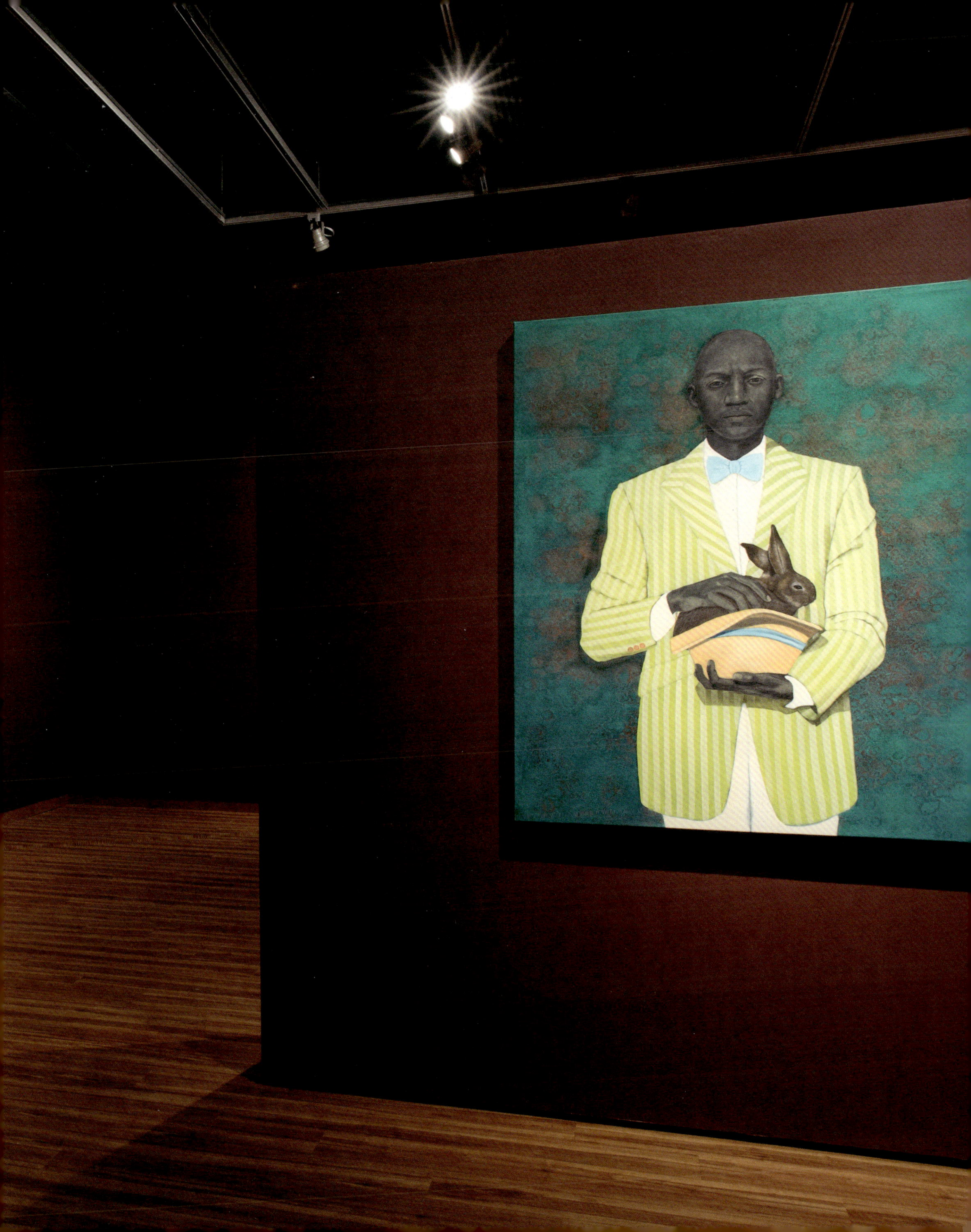

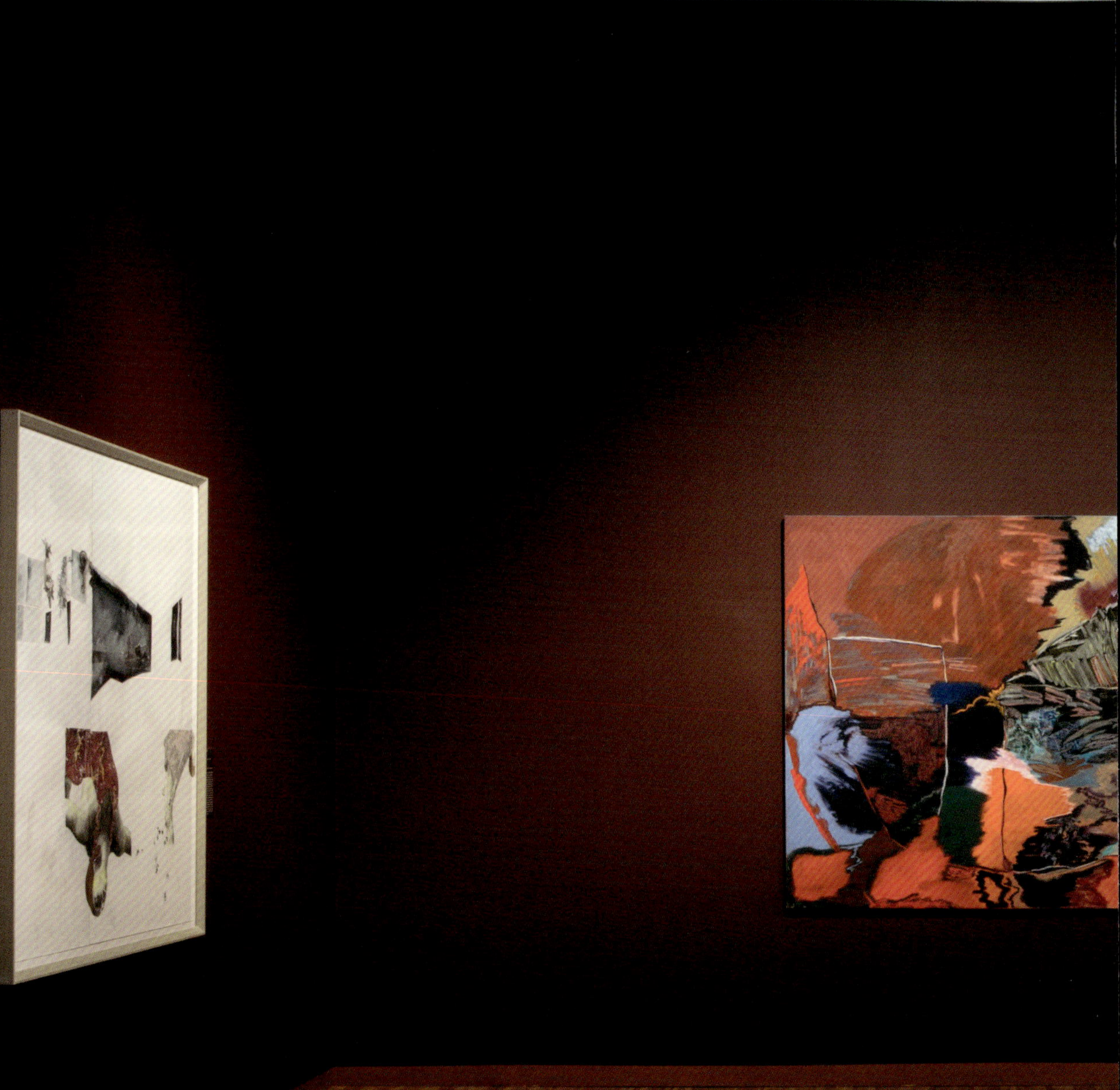

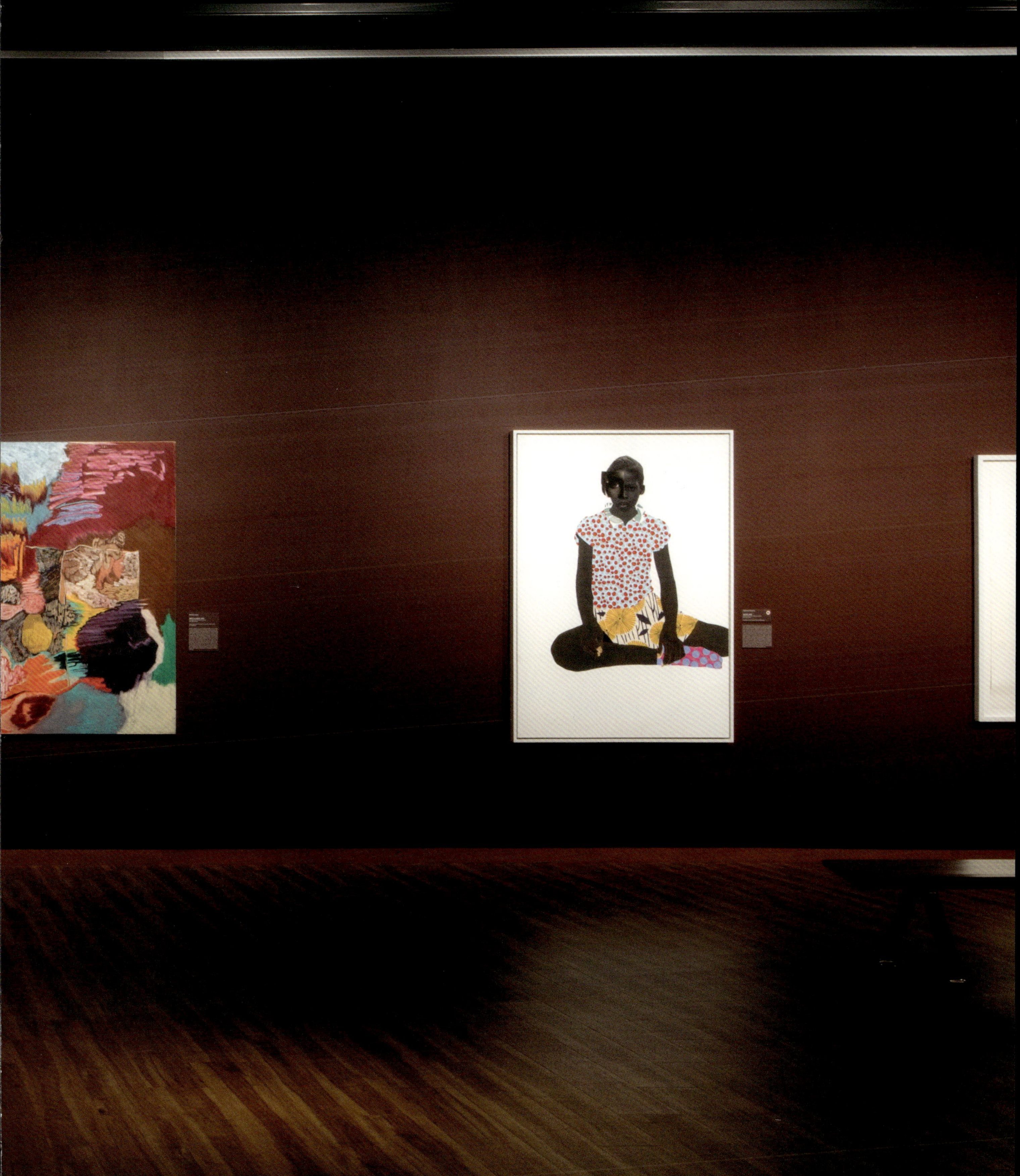

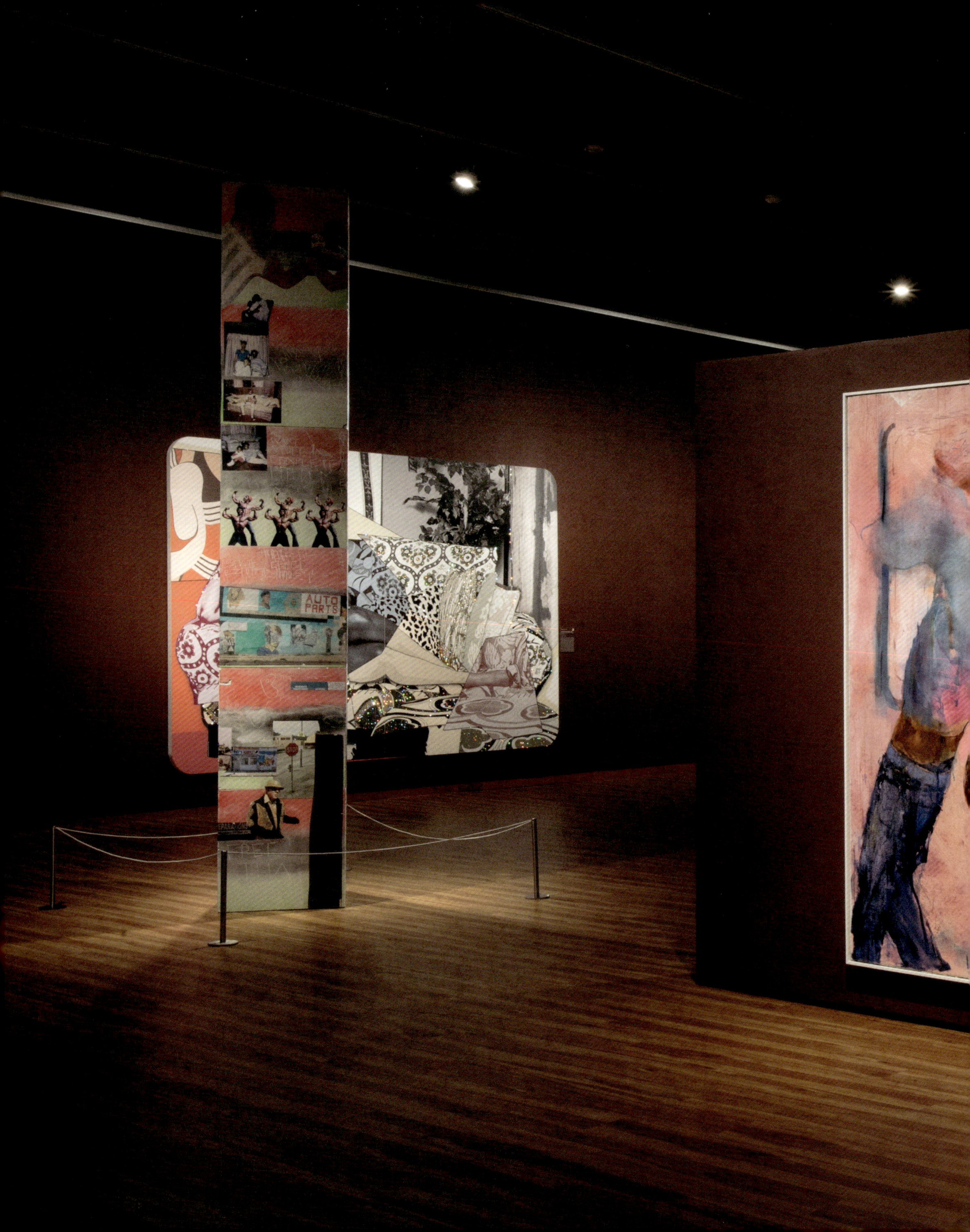

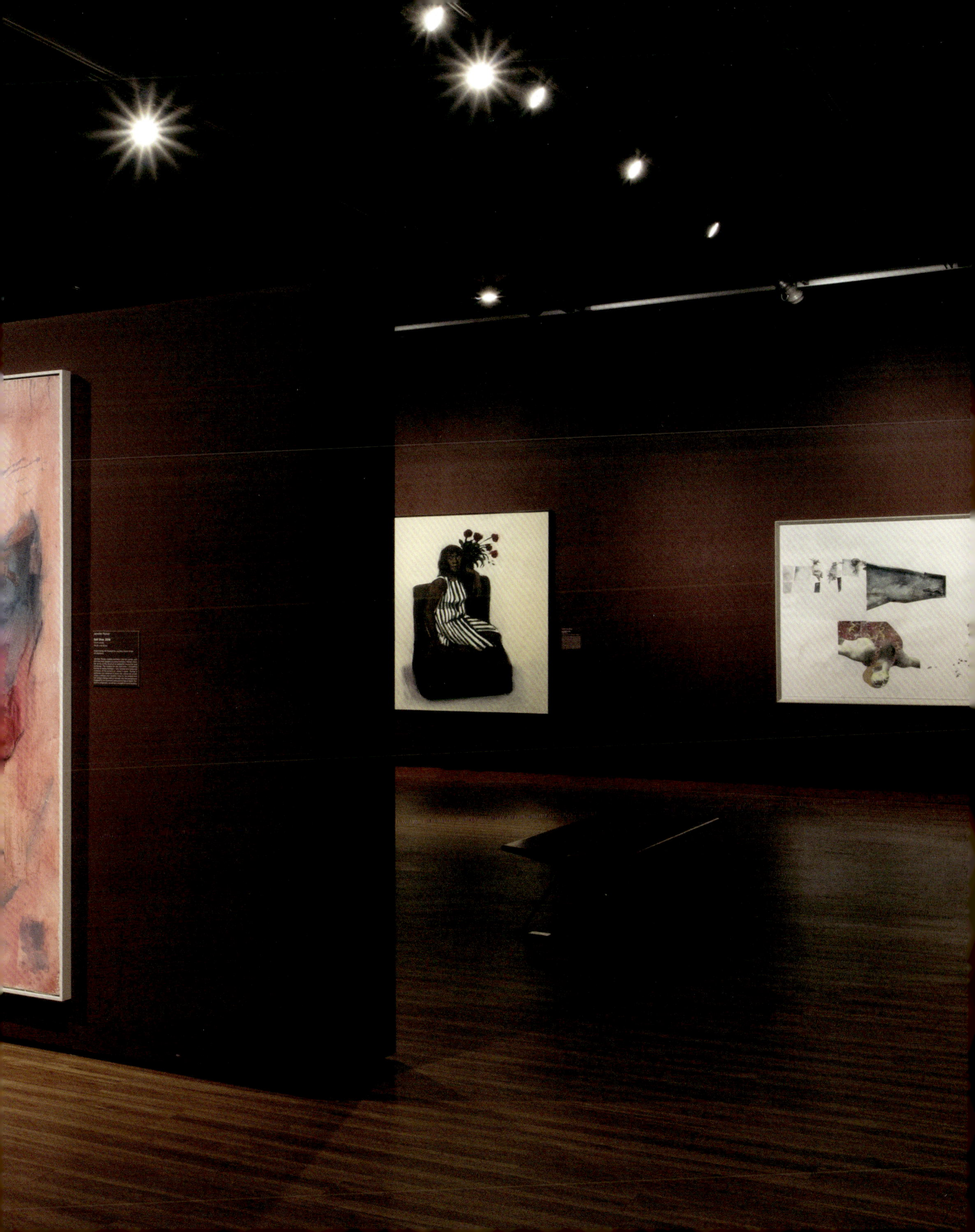

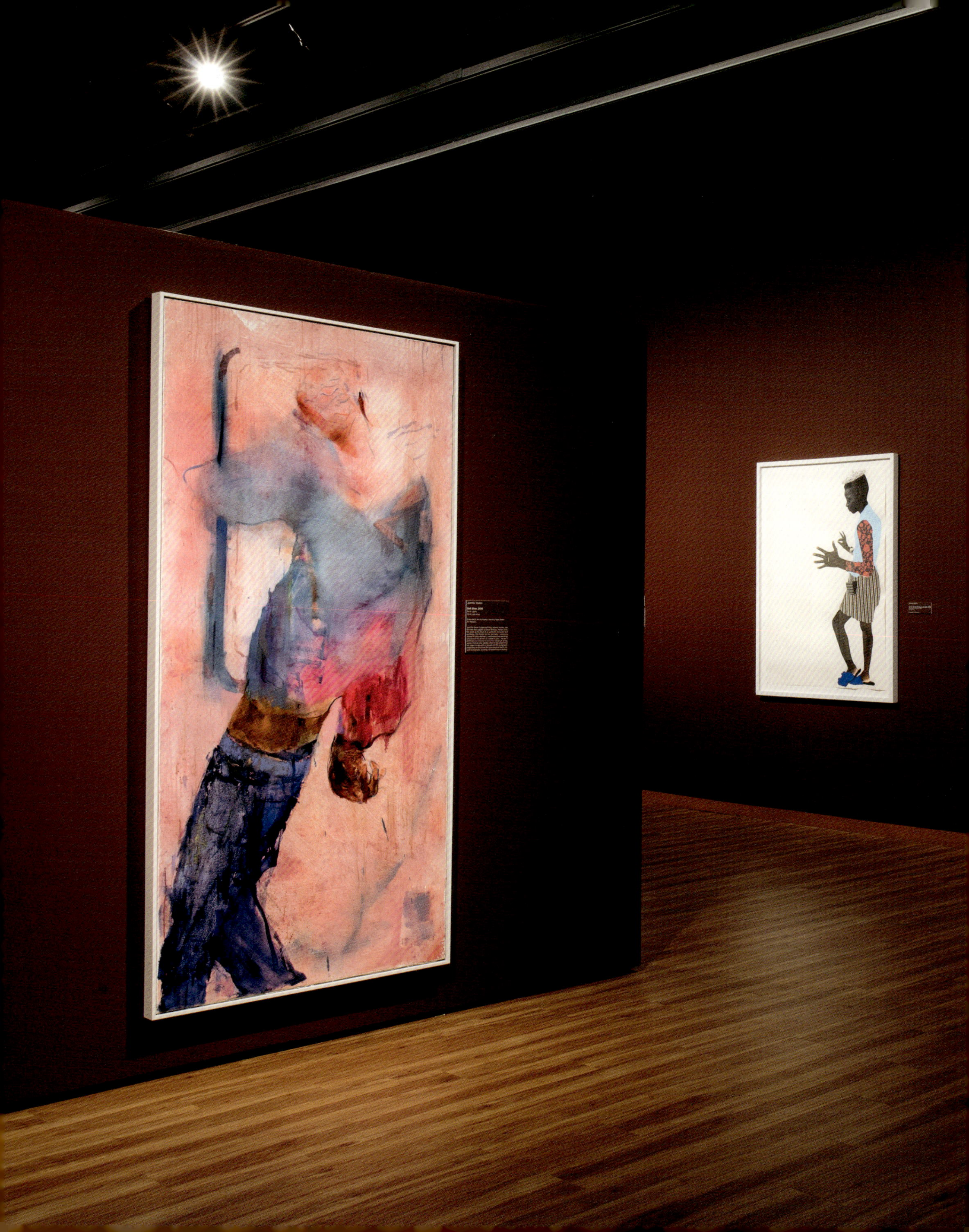

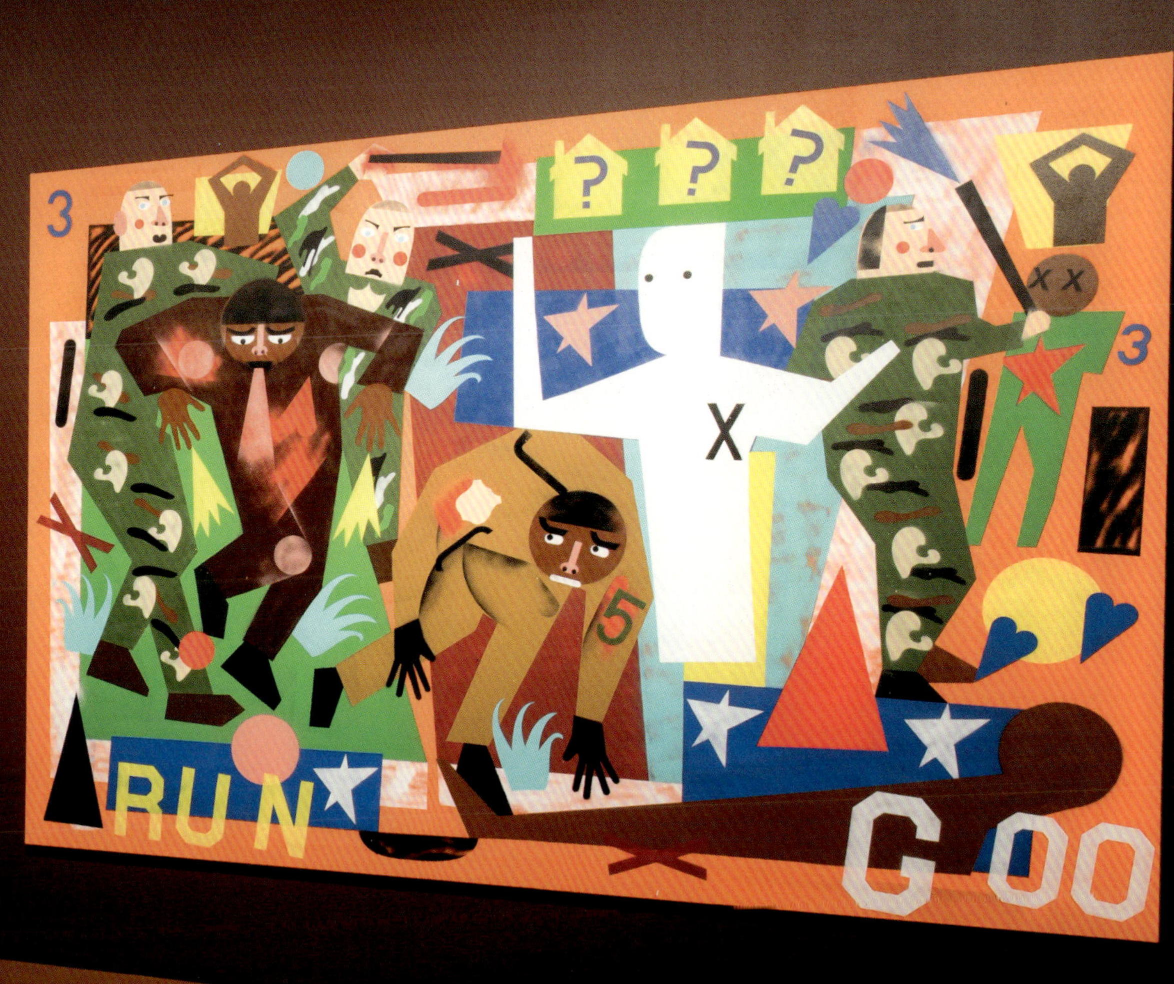
3
?
?
?
X
3
X
5
RUN
GOO

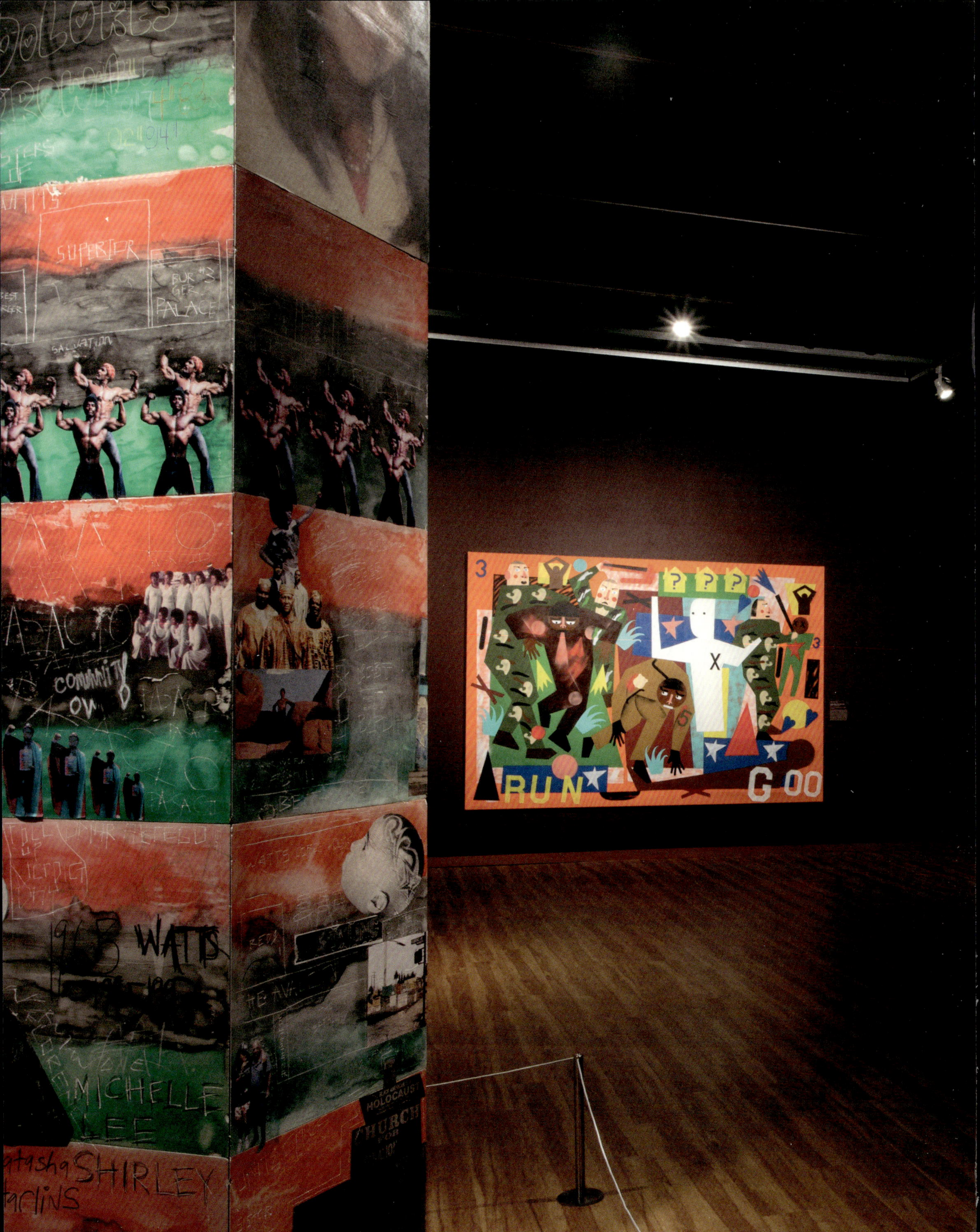

SUPERIER
BUR'S GER PALACE
SALVATION
COMMUNITY OW'D
WATTS
MICHELLE LEE
SHIRLEY
RUN
G OO
3
X

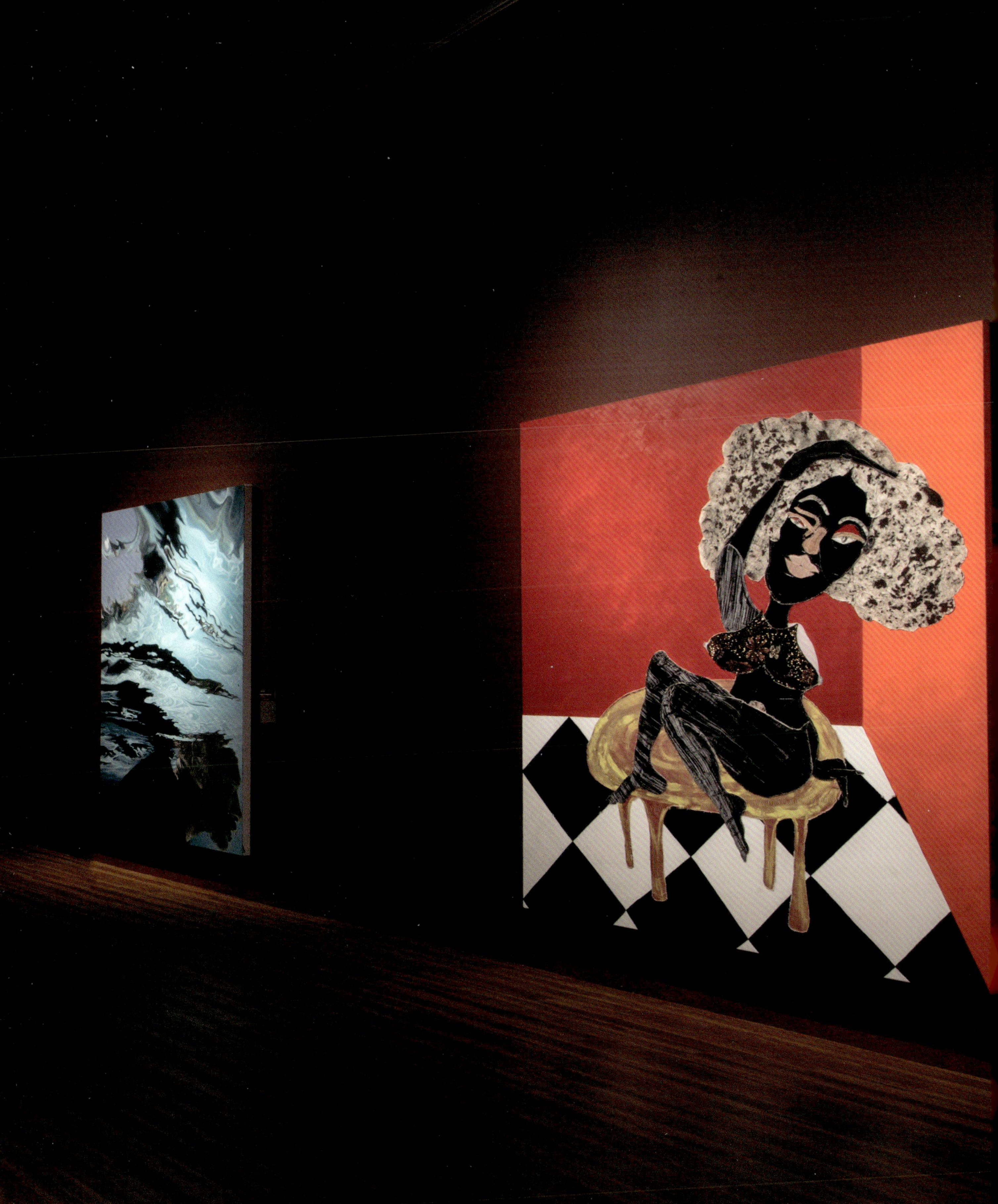

EXHIBITION CHECKLIST

NINA CHANEL ABNEY
Always Ready, Always There, 2018
Acrylic and spray paint on canvas
84⅛ × 120¼ × 1¾ inches

Green Family Art Foundation,
courtesy Adam Green Art
Advisory. © Nina Chanel Abney.
Courtesy of the artist and Jack
Shainman Gallery, New York.

ruby onyinyechi amanze
Dive Sky, 2020
Photo transfer, graphite, ink,
metallic enamel, gouache,
acrylic on paper
59 × 67 × 2 inches

Courtesy of the Collection
of Kelly and Adam Leight.

LAUREN HALSEY
WE IN HERE, 2022
Watercolor ink, colored pencil,
collage, and hand carving
on gypsum
140¾ × 23½ × 23½ inches

Courtesy of Kent & Tamara
Kelley. Images courtesy of
the artist and David Kordansky
Gallery. Photography by
Andy Romer / Allen Chen /
SLH Studio.

RACHEL JONES
SMIIILLLLEEEE, 2021
Oil pastel and oil stick on canvas
63 × 98½ inches

Green Family Art Foundation,
Courtesy Adam Green Art
Advisory. © Rachel Jones.
Courtesy of the artist and
Thaddeus Ropac.
Photo: Chad Redmon.

TOYIN OJIH ODUTOLA
By Her Design, 2017
Charcoal, pastel, and pencil
on paper
68 × 42 inches

©Toyin Ojih Odutola.
Courtesy of the artist and Jack
Shainman Gallery, New York.

JENNIFER PACKER
Soft Shoe, 2018
Oil on canvas
79¼ × 36 inches

Green Family Art Foundation,
courtesy Adam Green Art
Advisory. Artwork © Jennifer
Packer, courtesy of Sikkema
Jenkins & Co., New York;
Corvi-Mora, London.

CALIDA RAWLES
Requiem for my Navigator, 2021
Acrylic on canvas
96 × 72 × 2½ inches

Courtesy of the Shah Garg
Collection. © Calida Rawles.
Courtesy the artist and
Lehmann Maupin, New York,
Seoul, and London.
Photo by Marten Elder.

DEBORAH ROBERTS
Delilah, 2021
Mixed media and collage
on canvas
65 × 45 inches

Courtesy of the Forman Family
Collection. Copyright Deborah
Roberts. Courtesy the artist
and Stephen Friedman Gallery,
London and New York.
Photo: Paul Bardagjy.

DEBORAH ROBERTS
Let me tell you this again and again, 2020
Mixed media and collage
on paper
52 × 38 inches

Courtesy of Sarah Simmons.
Copyright Deborah Roberts.
Courtesy the artist and Stephen
Friedman Gallery, London and
New York.
Photo: Paul Bardagjy.

TSCHABALALA SELF
Red Room, 2022
Crushed velvet, fabric, acrylic,
flashe, spray paint, thread,
and painted canvas on canvas
94 × 84 × 1½ inches

Green Family Art Foundation,
courtesy Adam Green Art
Advisory. © Courtesy the
artist, Pilar Corrias, London,
and Galerie Eva Presenhuber,
Zurich / Vienna.

AMY SHERALD
The Rabbit in the Hat, 2009
Oil on canvas
54 × 43 × 2¾ inches

Green Family Art Foundation,
courtesy Adam Green Art
Advisory. © Amy Sherald.
Courtesy the artist and Hauser &
Wirth. Photography by Christina
Hussey @christinahussey.

MICKALENE THOMAS
Clarivel Face Forward Gazing, 2024
Rhinestones, acrylic, and oil
paint on canvas mounted on
wood panel
96 × 144 inches

Courtesy of the artist.

LYNETTE YIADOM-BOAKYE
6pm Madeira, 2011
Oil on canvas
70⅞ × 59 inches

Courtesy of the Collection
of Tracey and Phillip Riese.

DEXTER WIMBERLY

Dexter Wimberly is an American curator based in Japan who has organized exhibitions in galleries and institutions around the world, including the Museum of Arts and Design in New York City; the Green Family Art Foundation in Dallas, TX; the Harvey B. Gantt Center in Charlotte, NC; KOKI Arts and STANDING PINE in Tokyo, Japan; BODE in Berlin, Germany; Lehmann Maupin in London, UK; and the Third Line in Dubai, UAE. His exhibitions have been reviewed and featured in publications including the *New York Times* and *Artforum* and have received support from The Andy Warhol Foundation for the Visual Arts and the Kinkade Family Foundation. Wimberly is a Senior Critic at New York Academy of Art and the founder and director of the Hayama Artist Residency in Japan. He is also the cofounder and CEO of the online education platform CreativeStudy.

KALIA BROOKS, PhD

Kalia Brooks, PhD, is the Director of Programs and Exhibitions at NXTHVN, currently serving as the Interim Executive Director. She is responsible for the design and delivery of curatorial exhibitions, public programs, artist projects, community engagement initiatives, and the learning environment for the fellowship and apprenticeship programs. Her academic research covers art from the nineteenth century to the present, with an emphasis on emergent technologies and African American, transatlantic and diasporic cultures of the Americas. Brooks holds a PhD in Aesthetics and Art Theory from the Institute for Doctoral Studies in the Visual Arts. She is coeditor of *Women and Migration: Responses in Art and History* (Open Book Publishers, Cambridge, UK, 2019 and 2022). She has served as a consulting curator for the City of New York through the Department of Cultural Affairs and was an ex-officio trustee on the Board of the Museum of the City of New York during the de Blasio administration.

HARVEY B. GANTT CENTER BOARD OF DIRECTORS FY '24

JIM DUNN, PHD
Board Chair
Enterprise Executive Vice President & Chief People and Culture Officer
Atrium Health

RICHARD CARTER
Treasurer
President & CEO
Carter P.C.

ANN CAULKINS
Senior Vice President
Novant Health

JONI Y. DAVIS
Community Leader

JANET HANSON
Managing Director, Wealth & Retirement
Deloitte Consulting LLP

JONTE' HARRELL
Managing Partner
Ossian Capital

LOUIS HAWKINS
Managing Director, Employee Technology Support
Bank of America

BRANDON LANE
VP, Head of Corporate Real Estate
Duke Energy Brandon

MICHELLE LEE
Community Leader

RODNEY MCKENZIE
Executive Vice President, Control Executive Consumer and Small Business Banking
Wells Fargo Bank, N.A. Rodney

HARVEY B. GANTT CENTER MUSEUM STAFF

BONITA BUFORD
President & CEO

CHANEL M. DAVIS
Chief Experience Officer

INGRID TRAVIS JAMES
Director of Marketing & Communications

LEANDRA–JULIET KELLEY
Director of Collections & Curatorial Affairs

MARTIN J. MCNEESE
Director of Technology & Innovation

AJA ROBERTS
Director of Institutional Advancement

ASIA C. ZIMMERMAN
Facilities Manager

NICOLE S. BEVERLY
Educational Initiatives Manager

AFENI GRACE
Public Programs Manager

CARLA JARRETT
Visitor Experience & Museum Store Manager

DARIS YORK
Events Manager

JOCELYN STANLEY
Educational Initiatives & Public Programs Coordinator

RYAN HALEY THOMAS
Collections & Exhibitions Coordinator

ANGEL BUTLER
Digital Engagement Strategist

MATTHEW B. LONG
Digital Streaming & Video Engineer

JOHNATHAN ROBBINS
Digital Creative Video Strategist

CIVONNE RAY
Visitor Experience Senior Associate

KIRSTYN ALSTON
Visitor Experience Associate

Published by Pacific and the Harvey B. Gantt Center for African-American Arts + Culture

Pacific
70 Flushing Avenue
Ground Floor, Suite 1
New York, New York 11205
www.pacificpacific.pub

Harvey B. Gantt Center
for African-American
Arts + Culture
551 South Tryon Street
Charlotte, North Carolina
28202
www.ganttcenter.org

On the occasion of
*A Superlative Palette:
Contemporary Black Women Artists*
(January 26 – August 25, 2024)

Publication © 2024 Pacific and the Harvey B. Gantt Center for African-American Arts + Culture, Charlotte, North Carolina. All rights reserved.

A Shared Sensibility of the Black Feminine
© 2024 Kalia Brooks, PhD
All images featured in this catalogue are © 2024.

Contributors: Bonita Buford, President & CEO of the Harvey B. Gantt Center for African-American Arts + Culture; Dexter Wimberly, Curator of *A Superlative Palette: Contemporary Black Women Artists*; and Kalia Brooks, PhD

For Pacific
Design and Production: Pacific
Editor: Elizabeth Karp-Evans
Copyeditor: Sarah Stephenson
Printer: Conti Tipicolor
Typeface: Mrs Eaves

Artwork images are courtesy of: Nina Chanel Abney and Jack Shainman Gallery, New York; ruby onyinyechi amanze and Goodman Gallery (Johannesburg, Cape Town, London, New York); Lauren Halsey and David Kordansky Gallery. Photography by Andy Romer / Allen Chen / SLH Studio; Rachel Jones and Thaddeus Ropac. Photography by Chad Redmon; Toyin Ojih Odutola and Jack Shainman Gallery, New York; Jennifer Packer and Sikkema Jenkins & Co., New York; Corvi-Mora, London; Calida Rawles and Lehmann Maupin, New York, Seoul, and London. Photography by Marten Elder; Deborah Roberts and Stephen Friedman Gallery, London and New York. Photography by Paul Bardagjy; Tschabalala Self and Pilar Corrias, London, and Galerie Eva Presenhuber, Zurich / Vienna; Amy Sherald and Hauser & Wirth. Photography by Ryan Stevenson; Mickalene Thomas; and Lynette Yiadom-Boakye and Jack Shainman Gallery, New York and Corvi-Mora, London.

Installation images are courtesy of the Harvey B. Gantt Center for African-American Arts + Culture. Photography by Christina Hussey @christinahussey.

Special thanks to Dexter Wimberly; Bonita Buford; Leandra-Juliet Kelley, Director, Collections + Curatorial Affairs at the Harvey B. Gantt Center for African-American Arts + Culture; and Ryan Thomas, Collections + Exhibitions Coordinator at the Harvey B. Gantt Center for African-American Arts + Culture.

Thank you to the Collection of Kelly and Adam Leight; Collection of Tracey and Phillip Riese; Forman Family Collection; Green Family Art Foundation; Toyin Ojih Odutola and Jack Shainman Gallery, New York; Kent and Tamara Kelley; Mickalene Thomas; Sarah Simmons; and Shah Garg Collection for contributing to the exhibition.

No part of this publication may be reproduced or transmitted in any form or by any means, electronic or mechanical, including photocopying, recording, or by any information storage or retrieval system, without permission in writing from the copyright holders except by a reviewer who wishes to quote brief passages in connection with a review written for inclusion in a magazine, newspaper, or broadcast.

ISBN: 9781737599890

Organizational support for this exhibition has been provided by:

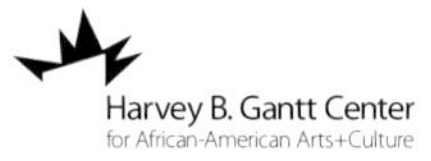

Initial support was provided from grants from the following organizations:

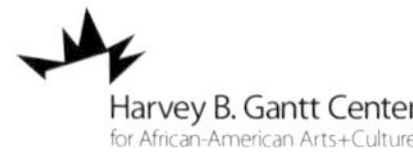

At Levine Center For The Arts
551 South Tryon Street
Charlotte, North Carolina
28202
704.547.3700
www.ganttcenter.org

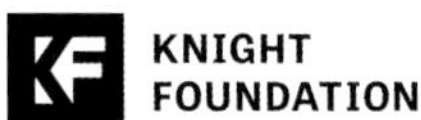
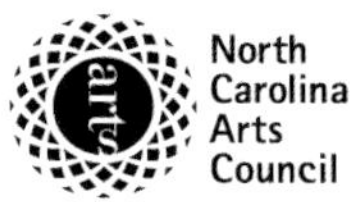
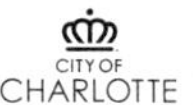 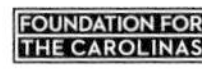

Harvey B. Gantt Center is supported, in part, by the Infusion Fund and its generous donors.

With generous support from:

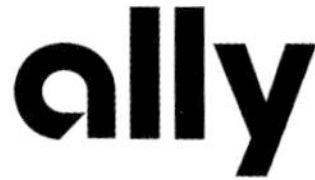

Get social with the Gantt Center @hbganttcenter

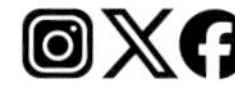